Monographic Journals of the Near East   *Afroasiatic Linguistics* 6/2 (December 1978)

T0153765

THE SAM LANGUAGES
A HISTORY OF RENDILLE, BONI AND SOMALI

by

Bernd Heine
Institut für Afrikanistik, Universität zu Köln

The Sam languages are spoken in the Eastern African countries of Somalia, Kenya and Ethiopia. They include Rendille, Boni and the various dialects of the Somali dialect cluster. The term "Sam" refers to a closely-knit unit of Cushitic languages within the Omo-Tana (formerly called "Somaloid" or "Macro-Somali") branch of Lowland East Cushitic. The Sam-speaking people originate from the Ethiopian Highlands. During the last two millennia, it is claimed here, they took possession of the arid plains of northeastern Kenya, Somalia and eastern Ethiopia. In the present paper an attempt is made at reconstructing aspects of the history of the Sam languages.

CONTENTS

1. INTRODUCTION

The present paper aims at describing some aspects of the linguistic history of a group of East African languages, i.e. Rendille, Boni, and Somali. At the same time it intends to provide some information on the early history of the people speaking these languages.

Our interest in the study of the Sam languages was aroused during field research within the project "Language Atlas of Kenya".[1] In the course of this, we were confronted with the task of documenting languages on which little or no information was available. Most of these languages turned out to belong to the East Cushitic branch of the Afroasiatic (Erythraic) family. When attempting to establish a genetic sub-classification we noticed that some of these East Cushitic languages differ considerably from each other in their structure and lexicon. The Yaaku (Mogogodo) language of central Kenya, for example, has been shown to belong to East Cushitic but it does not exhibit substantial similarities with other languages of this branch (see Greenberg 1963b; Ehret 1974:32-33). Other languages again share a relatively close genetic relationship. Such is the case with the Sam languages. This relationship has been largely ignored by scholars working on these languages, although Harold C. Fleming (1964) had drawn attention to it more than a decade ago.

Our field research revealed that it is possible to examine this relationship in more detail by applying the comparative method of historical linguistics. While some scholars have expressed doubts as to whether this method can be applied successfully to African languages outside the Bantu-speaking area, our comparisons within the Sam group suggest that these languages do not behave any differently from Bantu or Indo-European languages. The comparative method has been shown to be applicable to the Kuliak languages (Heine 1976a). The Sam languages constitute the second East African non-Bantu language unit to which this method proves to be applicable.

The notes that follow may suffer from a number of obvious shortcomings. Perhaps the most serious one is that the author is not a "Cushitist". With an academic tradition that goes back to the first half of the 19th century, Cushitic studies constitute one of the best established branches of Africanistics.[2] To familiarize oneself adequately with this field would require years of intensive study, yet the author must confess that he did not become interested in comparative Cushitic studies until 1975 when he was compelled to deal with Kenyan Cushitic languages as part of the project "Language and Dialect Atlas of Kenya".

Secondly, the linguistic materials on which this work is based are in most cases scanty, the only data on languages like Rendille and Boni available to date being shorter vocabularies and grammatical sketches.

Another shortcoming may be seen in the fact that a substantial amount of publications are available on one of the languages considered here, i.e. Somali. Thanks to the work of Leo Reinisch, Ernesto Cerulli, B.W. Andrzejewski and others, Somali has become one of the

---

[1]This project is sponsored by the *Deutsche Forschungsgemeinschaft*. It is conducted jointly by Wilhelm Möhlig, who is responsible for the Bantu languages, and the present author dealing with the non-Bantu languages of Kenya.

[2]As early as 1845, there was some literature on Cushitic languages available, including grammatical descriptions and vocabularies. The designation 'Cushitic' was introduced by 1858 (see Köhler 1975: 290).

best-documented languages of Africa. Yet we have decided to exploit this wealth of published data only to a limited extent so as not to bias the results of our analysis too
much in favour of one particular language. In this way we have tried to establish a
somewhat balanced basis of interlinguistic comparison, although we cannot be sure whether
the disadvantages of this approach do not outweigh its advantages.

It is nevertheless hoped that the present study may be of some use to people interested
in the languages and history of Cushitic-speaking peoples. It would seem to us that comparative research so far has been dominated by large-scale comparison involving many
divergent languages.[3] On the other hand, very little information is available on the
internal structure of various Cushitic sub-groups; more often, the existence of linguistic
relationships has been assumed rather than proven. One of the main goals of this paper is
therefore to encourage small-scale comparative research on Cushitic languages, with
particular emphasis on those languages that have hitherto largely escaped the attention of
scholars working in this field.

The present paper would not have been possible without the encouragement we received from
Hans-Jürgen Sasse. We are deeply indebted to him for his invaluable advice on all matters
relating to Cushitic studies. We would also like to express our gratitude to Derek
Elderkin who made available his unpublished field notes on Boni, to Max Trutenau who read
an earlier version of this paper and suggested various improvements, and to Robert Hetzron
for various critical comments.

2. THE SAM LANGUAGES

2.1. THE LANGUAGES

The following languages are included in this group:

2.1.1. Rendille[4]

The self-designation for the language is *af i rend'ille*. The Rendille-speaking people
inhabit the southern part of Marsabit District in Northern Kenya. According to the Kenya
Population Census of 1969, they number 18,729. The total of Rendille speakers, however,
must be assumed to be below 15,000 (see below).

Rendille society is divided on economic, social and geographical grounds into two sections:
the "Rendille proper", who have what is essentially a camel economy, and the Ariaal
(*ari'āāl*, Pl *ariaal'ō*). The "Rendille proper" occupy the northern part of the Rendille
country, i.e. the desert-like areas between Marsabit and the south-eastern shores of Lake
Turkana (formerly Lake Rudolf), whereas the Ariaal with their focus on cattle economy
inhabit the southern part of Rendille country, the Logologo-Laisamis area and a narrow
strip all along the northern fringes of Sampur country. Socio-economically, the Ariaal
Rendille occupy a position somewhere between the "Rendille proper" and the Sampur
(Samburu), their southern neighbours (Spencer 1973:130).

The difference between these two sections of Rendille society is also reflected in language behaviour (see Heine 1976a:1.3): whereas the majority of "Rendille proper" are

---

[3]We do not wish to underrate the relevance of such studies. Their importance has
only recently been demonstrated again in comparative work on the Cushitic verb conducted
by Robert Hetzron (1974) and Andrzej Zaborski (1975).

[4]For more detailed information on the language see Heine (1976b).

monolingual Rendille speakers, Ariaal society is marked by a pattern of bilingualism which
seems to lead to a language shift from Rendille to Sampur, an Eastern Nilotic language.
Nowadays, children usually grow up with Sampur as their first and primary language,
having hardly any knowledge of their parents' language. This is particularly so along
the southern fringes of Ariaal country. In Laisamis, the largest trading center of
southern Rendille, for example, Rendille has been found to be the first language of 83
per cent of the people over twenty years. Among the children under ten, on the other hand,
98 per cent speak Sampur as their first language.

Due to this process of language shift, there is a notable discrepancy between ethnic and
linguistic affiliation. There are probably several thousand young Ariaal people who
claim to be Rendille by tribe, but who speak Sampur, rather than Rendille, as their
first and primary language.

Until 1975, Rendille has been a virtually unknown language, the only published data on it
being those of Harold C. Fleming (1964:60-71), collected during several hours of informant-
work. In 1976, Heine published notes on Rendille grammar (Heine 1976a). Since then,
various more substantial contributions to our knowledge of Rendille have been made, in
particular Oomen (1977a; 1977b), Hudson (1977), and Sim (1977).

2.1.2. Boni[5]

The Boni (Aweera) language is spoken in the well-wooded hinterland of Lamu District in
Kenya between the Tana river and the Somalia boundary, with some groups extending into
southern Somalia. The Boni-speaking people consist of a few thousand hunters and gatherers[6]
who in recent years have begun to give up their traditional economy in favour of farming.

The Boni are called *waat^a* by the Galla, their western neighbours, *b'oon* by the Somali and
wa^{9}boni by the Swahili. There has been some confusion surrounding the term "Boni"
since it has been applied with reference to various other hunter-gatherer communities in
the area of the lower Tana, all of which are Galla-speaking.

A.N. Tucker (1969) therefore proposed to replace this name by "Aweera", which he claims
is the name by which the Boni refer to themselves. *aweer*, or *aweer-a*, is the Boni word
for 'hunter' or 'to hunt' and may refer to anybody engaged in the activity of hunting,
independent of his ethnic background. We have therefore proposed to return to the name
"Boni", mainly because of the following reasons: (a) this is the term being used by the
Kenyan administration, and (b) the Boni themselves seem to prefer to be referred to by
this name (Heine 1977c:1-3).

In order to avoid any further confusion, we shall henceforth reserve the name "Boni" to
the "true Boni" whose language is treated in this paper and refer to the other groups that
have been subsumed under this label either by their own names (e.g. *wáát many'óle, wáát
g'éde*) or else by the qualifying designation "Galla-speaking Boni".

---

[5]For more detailed information on the language see Heine (1977).

[6]The exact number of Boni speakers is not known. The Kenya Population Census of 1969
lists 3,972 "Boni/Sanye" as living in Kenya, and of these 1,276 are found in the Lamu
District where most Boni live, and 835 in Tana River District. Since these figures
include not only Boni but also some "Galla-speaking Boni" as well as the South Cushitic
Dahalo, one is lead to assume that the total number of Boni speakers may not exceed
2,000. There is no more recent information on the number of Boni living in Southern
Somalia.

Although the language is spoken by only a relatively small number of people, it can be subdivided into a number of clearly distinct dialects. The Boni themselves refer to the various dialect groups by the following names:

(a) *b'ireere²*   located in the west, in and around Pandanguo;

(b) *safar'êe²*   between Pandanguo and Mkunumbi;

(c) *ki'áângu²*   in the center, near the coast, around settlements like Baragoni, Ndununi and Magumba (Mwalimu);

(d) *k'ác̣e²*   in the northeast between Bodhei and Mararani in Milimani, Basuba (Bauri), and Mangai.

Even this list may not exhaust the number of possible Boni dialects, other group names being: (e) *kilii* and (f) *wayore*, both in Somalia around Kisimayu, (g) *bera*, living in roughly the same area as the *ki'áângu²* in Ndununi and Magumba, (h) *dura*, near Kiunga, and (i) *gedia*, near river Tana. The *kilii* are said to be mostly Somali-speaking and the *gedia* mostly Galla-speaking (Steve Harvey, personal communication of February, 1976).

Two short vocabularies published in the 19th century by G.A. Fischer (1878:141-144) and H.H. Johnston (1886:401-402), as well as a few grammatical notes (Tucker 1969:66-81) are the only published data on this language to date. An elaborate discussion on the 19th century vocabularies and on the position of Boni has been provided by Harold C. Fleming (1964:71-78). Our own account of the language (Heine 1977) is based on the western dialect (*b'ireere²*) but speakers of central and eastern Boni have been consulted as well.

2.1.3. "Jabarti"

It is neither known WHO speaks this language nor WHERE exactly it is spoken, nor whether it is STILL spoken anywhere today. The first account of it stems from Leo Reinisch who in 1904 published a short monograph, based on data collected by Wilhelm Hein during his expedition to Aden and Shekh Osman in 1901/1902 (Reinisch 1904). The other major contribution to the study of Jabarti was made by Maria von Tiling (1921/22) who was able to work with a "Jabarti" speaker in Hamburg.

The "Jabarti" inhabit the southern part of Somalia from 6° n.l. to approximately 3° n.l. along the coast as well as inland between the rivers Juba and Shebelle. "Jabarti" is a name given to them by the Arabs, their own name being unknown.[7] They are said to be divided into two main "tribes": the Digil and the Hawiyye (Hoye). Digil and Hawiyye belong to basically different congeries of clans: whereas the Hawiyye form one of the four main clan-families of the Samaale or Somali proper (the others being the Dir, Isaaq, and the Daarood; I.M. Lewis 1960:214/215), the Digil, together with the Rahanwiin, belong to the Sab, i.e. the second major part of the Somali nation which occupies the fertile lands between the Shebelle and the Juba rivers.[8]

From the few details given by Reinisch and von Tiling it would seem that the Jabarti overwhelmingly, if not exclusively, belong to the Sab. Maria von Tiling's informant

---

[7]For a discussion of the name, see Tiling 1921/22:20-22.

[8]Note that I.M. Lewis claims that both the Digil and Rahanwiin have been Galla-speaking until recently, and both are said to have arisen "from the intermixture of south-driving Somali with the rearguard of the Galla occupying most of the lower reaches of the Juba" (I.M. Lewis 1955:46). In the light of more recent research (see Ch. 5) it is doubtful whether this view is indeed in accordance with some historical developments in Southern Somalia.

Osman Abdi for example mentioned that the people referred to as "Jabarti" in Aden have a low standing, doing lowly jobs such as cleaning public lavatories and drains. Osman Abdi considered the term "Jabarti" as equivalent to low worker and ignorant person. He would insist that this does not apply at all to the Hawiyye. I.M. Lewis describes the Sab in the following way:

> "The Sab are held in contempt for their lowly origins, stemming from Sab as opposed to Somali, for their heterogeneous composition which includes Negroid elements, for their lack of a clear, politically significant genealogical structure, and, more importantly perhaps, because they are predominantly cultivators" (I.M. Lewis 1955:31).

From the distribution of the "Jabarti" it appears that they are, or have been, largely cultivators, differing from the pastoral Samaale living farther north and south.

Both Reinisch and von Tiling consider Jabarti a dialect of the Somali language, though von Tiling has some reservations. She talks of the "language of the Jabarti" and emphasizes that Jabarti differs considerably from Somali (1921/22:23) having been "separated from it a long time ago and forming a linguistic development area of its own" (1921/22:160). I.M. Lewis remarks on the difference between Sab and "Somali proper":

> "Linguistically the speech of the Sab differs from that of the northern pastoralists by about as much as French does from Italian. The gulf in language is thus much wider than that between any of the northern pastoral dialects" (Lewis 1961:13).

Assuming that "the speech of the Sab" is more or less identical with "Jabarti" there would seem to be some justification in treating Jabarti and Somali as different languages, which, however, belong to one and the same dialect continuum—in a similar way as French and Italian do. In more recent times, Jabarti has been influenced considerably by Somali, i.e. the language of the Samaale or "Somali proper".

2.1.4. Somali

Somali is by far the most important of all the Sam languages. The name of the language is *af soomáali*. The total of its speakers exceeds three millions. Most of them live in the Republic of Somalia where Somali is both the national and the official language. Other areas inhabited by Somali are the Northeastern Province as well as the Tana river area of Kenya, the Harar region of Ethiopia, and French Somaliland. For the literature on Somali, see Johnson (1963).

Somali is divided into a number of dialects which seem to form a large dialect continuum. A satisfactory description of this continuum has not yet been presented to date. The Handbook of African Languages, following B.W. Andrzejewski, the outstanding Somali scholar, lists three main dialect groups, which may be referred to as the Northern, Southern, and Benadir groups, respectively.[9] The Northern dialects are spoken by the typically pastoral Isaaq, Daarood, Dir and Hawiyye (Hawiya, Hoye), i.e. those clan-families which according to I.M. Lewis make up the Samaale or "Somali proper" (I.M. Lewis 1961:12). The Southern dialects include the Rahanwiin and probably the Tuuni and Jiddu. The Benadir (*banáadir*) speaking people are said to consist of the "largely detribalized inhabitants of the coastal towns of Somalia" (Tucker/Bryan 1956:125-26).

---

[9]Note that these terms are based on historical considerations (see Ch. 5). Due to more recent migrations, some sections of Northern clan-families are now found living to the south of the Southern dialect area (5.6).

2.1.5. Other Sab Languages

Apart from "Jabarti", there are two more linguistically divergent "tribes" belonging to the Sab section of Somali. They are the Yibir and the Midgan.[10] J.W.C. Kirk remarks about them:

> "The *Yibirs* are said to be sorcerers, and to have prophetic powers and the power of cursing. They live by begging, but expecially by the levy of a tax on Somalis, at a marriage or the birth of a child .... The *Midgans* are by nature hunters or trappers, and live largely by the meat of game they can kill in the jungle. They are also employed by Somalis to work for them, in return for which they receive occasional payment, in food or otherwise, and protection, from their employer. This work consists in fetching wood, drawing water, and digging and cleaning wells.
>
> Both tribes also work in leather, tanning hides, and making leather orna-ments, saddles, shoes, etc." (Kirk 1905:184).

These two tribes are said to speak languages that, although being structurally similar to Somali, differ in their lexicon considerably both from Somali and from each other. The data published by Kirk (1905) suggest that they might be artificial codes rather than being natural languages.[11] The scanty evidence available does not allow for any clear-cut statement on the genetic position of these languages.

2.2. CLASSIFICATION

The Sam languages belong to the Cushitic sub-family of the Afroasiatic (Erythraic) lan-guage family. Within Cushitic, the genetic position of Sam can be described by means of the following tree diagram (cf. Bender et al. 1976:14; 43):

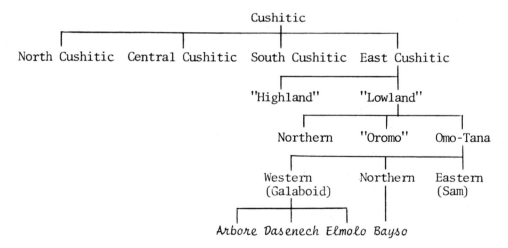

---

[10]Note that although these two groups are commonly referred to as "Sab" they have to be distinguished from the Digil and Rahanwiin, both on diachronic and synchronic grounds (cf. I.M. Lewis 1961:14).

[11]Kirk mentions with respect to Midgan: "In account, given me by a Midgan, of the traditional origin of his tribe, it was suggested that this language was invented by the Midgan's ancestors in the jungle as a secret code" (Kirk 1905:189-90).

The Sam languages, which form the Eastern sub-group of Omo-Tana, are sub-classified in the following way (see Heine 1976b:3):

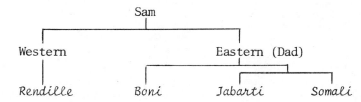

The above classification differs in some ways from previous classifications, especially in the following points:

(1) The term "Omo-Tana" is new, it replaces earlier designations like "Macro-Somali" (Fleming 1964) and "Somaloid" (Bender 1971) which do not seem justifiable on linguistic grounds (see Heine 1976b).

(2) The Galaboid languages Arbore, Dasenech and Elmolo, which were allocated to the southern branch of "Oromo" in Fleming (1976:43), are classified as Omo-Tana languages on the basis of recent evidence presented by Hans-Jürgen Sasse (1975).

(3) The classification of the Sam languages largely agrees with that proposed by Harold C. Fleming (1964:82-83), but differs from that contained in Fleming (1976:43), which considers Rendille, Boni, Rahanwiin, Southern Somali and Northern Somali as co-ordinate members of one and the same group, i.e. Sam. Evidence in favour of the present classification is contained in Ch. 4 of this paper.

(4) A particularly close relationship between Elmolo and the Sam languages had been claimed in Heine (1973). More recent studies suggest that Elmolo has to be excluded from the list of Sam languages after all.

The term "Sam" is derived from the root *ʂam common to the languages of this group.[12]

3. PROTO-SAM

The present section presents an attempt at "reconstructing" characteristics of the hypothetical ancestor language of the modern Sam languages, called "Proto-Sam".[13]

Although it is the aim of the following paragraphs to provide a general outline of the assumed proto-language there are various important aspects of structure that will not be

---

[12] The same root occurs in other phonological shapes (e.g. *ʂoono, ʂunan*) in other East Cushitic languages (also *ʂssân* in Awngi). H.J. Sasse (personal communication) suggests that the reconstructed form should be *ʂan, rather than *ʂam. On the basis of evidence from Somali and other Eastern Cushitic languages, this appears to be a plausible claim. On the other hand, one may postulate a change Proto-Sam *ʂam > Somali ʂan, pl. ʂan-an (< *ʂam-an) as a result of regressive assimilation, Somali having a general rule $m \rightarrow n/$ ___ #. It would seem that this is a slightly more obvious explanation than assuming that Rendille underwent a change *ʂan > *ʂam.

[13] Note that the term "ancestor language" is not, and cannot be, meant in a literal sense. Since we have no records whatsoever of it, all "reconstructions" must remain hypothetical, i.e. they cannot be considered as actually spoken linguistic forms.

discussed. For example, Proto-Sam must have had a case system marked by nominal suffixes,
yet the reader will find hardly any information on this phenomenon. Similarly, neither
a treatment of tonal structure nor of verbal modality patterns is provided. The main
reason for omitting such aspects of language structure is either that the data available
on the various languages are not sufficient, or else that these languages differ from each
other so much that a comparative analysis of the relevant structures does not seem
possible.

The linguistic materials presented in this section have been taken from the following main
sources: Heine (1976b) for Rendille; Heine (1977) for Boni; von Tiling (1921/22) for
Jabarti; Kirk (1905), Bell (1953) and Tucker/Bryan (1966) for Somali. The reader is
referred to these for further information. In addition, unpublished data on Boni collected
by Derek Elderkin have been utilized. The transcription used is summarized in Table 1.

The following abbreviations will be used:

    B   Boni
    E   eastern and central Boni dialects
    Ed Boni data collected by Derek Elderkin
    F   Feminine gender
    J   Jabarti
    M   Masculine gender
    n   noun
    Pl plural
    R   Rendille
    S   Somali
    Sg singular

3.1. Phonology

See p. 11 for Table 1.

TABLE 1
TRANSCRIPTION

CONSONANTS

	Bilab.	Lab.-dent.	Dent.	Alv.	Post-alv.	Alv.-pal.	Pal.	Vel.	Uvul.	Glott.	Phar.
Plosive			*t*			*c*		*k*	*q*	ʔ	ʕ
	b		*d*		*ɖ*	*j, dʒ*		*g*			
Implosive	’*b*			’*d*			’*j*	’*g*			
Ejective			*t’*			*c’*		*k’*			
Fricative		*ɓ*	*θ*	*s*		*sh*		*x*		*h*	*ħ*
	β		*ð*	*z*					*ɣ*		
Lateral				*l*							
Roll				*r*	*ɽ*						
Nasal	*m*		*n*				*ny*	*ŋ*			
Glide	*w*						*y*				

VOWELS

Short vowels	*i, e, a, o, u*
Long vowels	*ii, ee, aa, oo, uu*
Semi-mute vowel	*e*

TONES

High	*á*	
High-falling	*â*	
Low	*a*	(i.e. unmarked; in reconstructed forms: *ã)
Accent	’*a*	

3.1.1. Consonants

*b

There is a series of mutually corresponding voiced bi-labial stops for which a Proto-Sam phoneme *b is set up. Rendille and Boni *b* has a fricative allophone [β] in intervocalic position.

      R *b’ēēn* F : S *been-ta* : B *b’ēe* F 'lie (n)'
      R *bic’ē* M : S *biiyo-hi* : J *biiyōō-gi* : B *biy’o* M 'water'
      R *xob’ōb* F 'cold (n)' : S *qaboob-hi* 'cold weather' : B *ab’ōob* M 'coolness'

*c

The voiceless alveolo-palatal stop *c* of Rendille corresponds to the fricative *sh* in all other Sam languages in morpheme-initial position. We derive this series from a hypothetical proto-phoneme *c.

R *cân* F : S *shan-ta* : J *shaŋ* : B *shâŋ* 'five'
R *cimbir* F : S *shimbir-ta* : B *sh'imir* F 'bird'
R *cel'ê* : S *sheley, shalei* : B *shâlᵉ* 'yesterday'

Another series R *c* : S *y* : J *y* : B *y* is confined to the intervocalic position within morphemes. It can be assumed that this series, too, derives from Proto-Sam *c* occurring between vowels. The former series does not occur in this environment.

R *bic'ê* M : S *biiyo-hi* : J *biiyôô-gi* : B *biy'o* M 'water'
R *ice* : S *iyâ-da* : J *iyye* 'she'
R *ico* : S *iyâ-da* : J *iyyoo* : B *iyo* 'they'

*d

The morpheme-initial dental stop *d* of Rendille, Somali and Jabarti corresponds to *t* in Boni. These phonemes can be said to go gack to a reconstructed phoneme *d*.

R *dub* 'to roast' : S *dub-an* 'roasted' : B *tûb* 'to roast'
R *dîm* M : S *diin-ki* : B *tiŋ* M (Ed) 'tortoise'
R *dab* M : S *dab-ka* : B *tôb* M 'fire'

Following vowels, all languages including Boni have a voiced dental phoneme *d* which may be realized as a fricative [ð].

R *d'iid* : S *diid* : B *t'iid* 'to refuse'
S *ᶜiddi-da* : B *idd'i* F 'fingernail', 'claw'
R *anx'âd* M 'lightning' : S *onkod-ki* 'thunder'

*ḍ

The post-alveolar voiced plosive *ḍ* of Rendille, Somali and Jabarti corresponds to an implosive alveolar stop *'d* in Boni. A proto-phoneme *ḍ* is postulated for this series.

R *ḍôg* F : S *ḍêg-ta* : J *ḍêg-ti* : B *'deg* F 'ear'
R *ḍîg* M : S *ḍiig-ga* : J *ḍiig-ti* : B *'diig* M 'blood'
R *ḍêr* : S *ḍer* : J *ḍeer* (high) : B *'d'êer* 'long'

Morpheme-internally after vowels, Boni has usually *r* corresponding to both *ḍ* and *ḍḍ* in the other Sam languages.

R *ħiḍ* : S *ħiḍ* : J *hir* : B *hir* 'to close, shut, tie'
S *foḍi* : B *foorᵉ* 'to whistle'
R *ħ'êêḍi* : S *ᶜeeḍin* : B *eer'i* 'unripe'

In Jabarti the post-alveolar voiced plosive *ḍ* has been replaced by a post-alveolar liquid *r* except in initial position (cf. von Tiling 1922: 38-39):

R *jîḍ* M 'meat' : S *jiḍ-ka* : J *jir* 'body'
S *feeḍ-da* : B *f'êe'd*, Pl *feerᵉ'* F/Pl : J *feer* 'rib'
R *'âḍi* M : S *aḍi-gi* : B *'irᵉ* M : J *iri* 'sheep and goats'

*f

All Sam languages have a labio-dental voiceless fricative which can be assumed to be derived from a proto-phoneme *f*.

R *fâr* M : S *far-ta* : J *far* : B *far* F 'finger'
R *fur* : S *fur* : B *fur* 'to open'
R *lâf* F : S *laf-ta* : B *laf* 'bone'
R *kuf* : S *kuf* : B *kûf* 'to fall'

*g

Rendille, Somali and Jabarti have a morpheme-initial voiced velar stop *g* corresponding to a voiceless velar stop *k* in Boni.

R *gey* M : S *geid-ki* : J *geed* : B *k'ēe* M 'tree'
R *garg'ar* : S *gargar* : B *kark'ar-s* 'to help'
S *ga^caan-ti* : J *gāaŋ* : B *k'ā'an* F 'hand, arm'
R *gûb* : S *gub* : B *kûb* 'to burn'

This series also occurs following *r*, e.g.

R *'āgar/'ārga* : S *arag* : B *ârk* 'to see'
(see also 'to help' above)

In non-initial position after vowels all languages, including Boni, have *g* as their reflex of *g*.

R *dîg* M : S *diig-ga* : J *diig-ti* : B *'diig* M 'blood'
R *m'āgañ* M : S *maga^ca* : B *m'ā^ɔag* M 'name'
R *nûg* : S *nuug* : B *n'ûug* 'to suck from breast'

The same applies to the environment following *g*:

R *m'ûgdi* M : S *mugdi-gi* (Mogadishu) : B *m'ûgde* M (E) 'darkness'

There is another series of correspondences R *j* : S *j* : Boni *sh* which is found only pre-ceding high front vowels. It would seem that there is some justification for considering this series as being derived from a proto-sound *[dʒ] which itself was an allophone of *g* occurring before *i*.

R *j'ilib* M : S *jilib-ka* : B *sh'ilub* M 'knee'
R *jit* F : S *jid-ki* : B *shid* M 'road, path'
R *jit* : S *jiid* : B *shiid* 'to pull'
R *jēbi* : S *jibi* 'to break (tr.)' (< *giābi*)

Morpheme-internally between vowels, *g* seems to have disappeared in Boni, as far as the following examples suggest:

R *g'ûgañ* M : B *kûa'* M 'clap of thunder'
R *agis/igis* : B *iis/iaas* 'to kill' (cf. 3.6.4.2)

*h

A glottal fricative *h can be reconstructed for the series R *h* : S *h* : B *h*.

R *hel* : S *hel* : B *hel* 'to get'
R *hor* 'first, earlier' : S *hor-ta* 'in front, firstly': B *hor-tēēd* 'past'
R *hāɬar* M : B *haɬ'ar* M 'wind'

Rendille has lost *h morpheme-initially in a number of cases. The conditions of this loss are unclear.

R *aa* : S *haa* : B *haa* 'yes'
R *ab'ar* : S *habaar* : B *hab'ar* (E) 'to curse'
R *or'ēi* 'in front' : S *horei* 'to be in front' ; B *hōr^ɔ* 'in front'

In intervocalic and morpheme-final positions, *h has become *ħ in Rendille, i.e. it has merged with *ħ.

R *soħ* : S *sooh* : B *sooh* (ED) 'to twist'
R *waħ'āl* : S *wehel* 'companion'
R *dañ* : S *deh* (Imper.) : B *erah* (Ed) 'to say'

*ħ

The voiceless pharyngal fricative *ħ* of Rendille and Somali corresponds to a glottal fricative *h* in Boni and Jabarti in morpheme-initial position. For this series, a Proto-Sam phoneme *ħ is reconstructed.

R ħiy M : S ħidid-ki : B h'ĩid M 'root'
S ħiddig-ta : J ħittig-i : B hiddē F 'star'
R ħat : S ħad : B had 'to steal'
R ħiɗ : S ħiɗ : B hir : J hir̥ 'to close, shut, tie'
S ħun : J huŋ 'bad'

In positions other than morpheme-initially *ħ is reflected as a glottal stop ' in Western Boni and as h elsewhere in the Boni-speaking area (E).

R orr'āħ F : B 'ōra' F; 'ōrah F (E) 'sun'
R raħ M : S raħ-a : B ra' M; rah M (E) 'frog'
S masqaħ-da : B miska' F; m^eskah F (E) 'brain'

Somali has lost *ħ in most cases if preceded and followed by *a:

S laas-ka : B l'āhas M 'well (of water)'
R -aħa : S -aa : J -aa : B -aha ; -a³ 'your (Sg poss.)'

*k

In morpheme-initial position, all Sam languages have a regularly corresponding voiceless velar plosive k for which a proto-phoneme *k is set up.

R k'āle(y) : S kaalei, kaalay : B k'āāl^e 'come!'
R kôr : S kor-i : B kor 'to climb'
R kôw : S kow-da : J kow : B kôw 'one'

Morpheme-internally following vowels Rendille k corresponds to g in all other Sam languages.

R uk'aħ F : S ugaħ-i : J ogāh 'egg'
R i-c'êk : S sheeg; sheg 'to tell'

If *k is followed by *i its reflex in Boni is sh:

S kilkilo-di : B shish'il F 'armpit'
S buk-i : B bushi- 'to be sick'

There is one seeming counter-example to this rule:

R k'iħi 'to wake up' : S ki^ci 'to awaken' : B k'ĩ³i 'to wake up'

This set of cognates appears to be derived from a Proto-Sam root *ka³ 'to stand up' (see 3.6.5.2.2).

In Jabarti, *k is reflected as sh if the following vowel is either i or e (see von Tiling 1922:49):

S keen : B k'ēe/k'ēena³ : J sheeŋ 'to bring'
R kel'êi : S keli-di (adj.) : J shêlee 'alone'
S barki-gi 'wooden pillow' : B bark^e F : J barshi 'headrest'

*l

There is a consonant l corresponding between all Sam languages for which a proto-phoneme *l is reconstructed.

R il F : S il (-sha) : J il : B îl F 'eye'
R gêl : S gal : B kal 'to enter'
R liħ : S liħ-da : J lih; li : B li³ 'six'
R lāf F : S laf-ta : S laf 'bone'

In a number of cases, Boni has lost word-final *l. The conditions under which this has happened are not known.

R *mind'íla* F 'shaving knife' : S *mandiíl* (-*sha*) 'knife' : B *míind* F; *mínn^e* (E) 'knife'
R *tum'âl* F : S *tumaal-ka* : B *t'úma* M 'blacksmith'

*m

All Sam languages have a nasal *m* which can be assumed to be derived from Proto-Sam *m.

R *mat'añ* M : S *madañ-a* : J *mádi'* : B *m'âta'* M 'head'
R *mín* M : J *míŋ* : B *mîŋ* M 'house'
R *maal'ím* M : *maalin-ta* : B *m'âál^e* F 'day'

Word-finally, there is a series R *m* : S *n* : J *ŋ* : B *n* (*ŋ* if the word is a Masculine noun) which can be said to be derived from Proto-Sam *m as well

R *rum* F : S *run-ti*, Pl *tumo-hi* : B *rûn* F 'truth'
R *tûm* 'to pound' : S *tun* 'to grind, geld' : B *tun* 'to pound'
R *xáálim* M 'young male camel' : S *qaalin-ki*, Pl *qaalimo-hi* 'larger male calf'
R *lux'úm* F : S *luqun-ti* Pl *luqumo-hi* 'neck'
S *ga^caan-ti*, Pl *ga^caamo-hi* : J *gáâŋ* : B *k'â^ɔan* F 'hands, arm'

In the above examples, Somali has *n* if either a consonant or a word boundary follows and *m* if a vowel follows. There are, however, other words where even with preceding vowels Somali *n* corresponds to Rendille *m*:

R *gac'âm* M : S *gashan-ki*, Pl *gashano-di* 'shield'
R *sâm* M : S *san-ka*, Pl *sanan* : B *saŋ* M 'nose'

It would seem that in these cases the rule *m* → *n*/__# has been extended to the morpheme-final position although it is unclear why this has not happened throughout the language, e.g. in words like Somali *run-ti*, *rumo-hi* 'truth' (see above).

Boni has lost *m in intervocalic position. This development appears to have affected Prefix-Verbs only (cf. 3.6.4.2; 4.1).

R *imi(t)* 'to arrive' : S *im-an* : B *iid/iaad* 'to come'
R *amut* : B *uud/uaad* 'to die'

*n

All Sam languages have a nasal *n* which can be traced back to a proto-phoneme *n.

R *nañas* M : S *naas-ka* : B *n'â^ɔas* M 'female breast'
R *nûg* : S *nuug* : B *n'úug* 'to suck'
R *m'áánta* : S *maanta* : B *m'âan* 'today'

Word-finally, *n is reflected in Jabarti as *ŋ*. In Boni, it is usually retained as *ŋ* in the case of Masculine nouns and lost in other cases.

R *mín* M : J *míŋ* : B *mîŋ* M 'house'
R *wên* : S *wein*; *weyn* : J *wiiŋ* : B *wit/wiin-* 'big'
R -*iina* : S -*iin* : J -*iiŋ* 'your (Pl poss.)'
R *keen* : B *k'êe/k'éêna* 'to bring'
S *ñun* : J *huŋ* 'bad'
R *b'êên* F : S *been-ta* : B *b'êe* F; *b'êen* F (E) 'lie (n)'
R *bun* M 'coffee bean' : S *bun-ka* 'coffee' : B *bûŋ* M 'coffee bean'

In other cases again, word-final *n* has been retained in Boni:

S *dañan-ti* : B '*dah'an* F 'cold (n)'
R *xan'în* : S *qaniin* : B *an'ìin* 'to bite'
R *mañ'ân* F : B *mah'ân* F 'barren woman'

*q

A series of corresponding phonemes R x : S q : J q : B φ in word-initial position is
assumed to be derived from Proto-Sam *q, a voiceless uvular plosive.

    R x'óro M : S qori-gi : J gori : B 'or^e M 'wood, firewood'
    R xût : S qod-i : B od 'to dig, cultivate'
    R xât : S qaad : B 'âad 'to take'
    R x'âbo : S qabo : B 'ôbo 'to catch, hold'

In non-initial position following vowels, the correspondences are R x : S q : J g : B ' .

    R mindax'âr : S mindiqir-ka : B minî''ir 'intestines'
    R max'âl : S maqal-shi 'young goats and sheep'
    S maqal : B m'â'al 'to hear'
    S boqol-ki : J bogôl 'hundred'

*r

All Sam languages have a phoneme r which corresponds regularly between them. A proto-
phoneme *r is set up for this series.

    R far M : S far-ta : J far : B far F 'finger'
    R war'âba M : S waraabe-ha : J waraabâ-gi : B war'âa M 'hyena'
    R rum F : S run-ti : B rûn F 'truth'

*s

There is a phoneme s in all languages which is to be considered as a reflex of Proto-Sam *s.

    R sañ F : S sa^c-a : J saa' : B sâ' F 'cow'
    R s'îi : S sii : B sîi 'to give'
    R ñus'ûb : S ^cusub 'new' : B 'usub F 'newness'
    R nañas M : S naas-ka : B n'â'as M 'female breast'

*t

All Sam languages have a phoneme t in morpheme-initial position which can be said to be
derived from a proto-phoneme *t.

    R tim F : S tin-ka : J tin 'hair'
    R tom'ôn : S tooban-ki : J tumôŋ : B tam'ân 'ten'
    R tum'âl F : S tumaal-ka : B t'ûma M 'blacksmith'

Morpheme-internally following vowels, Rendille has t which corresponds to d in all other
Sam languages.

    R k'ati F : S kaadi-di : B k'ââd^e F 'urine'
    R mat'añ M : S madañ-a : J mâdi' : B m'âda' M 'head'
    R xût : S god-i : B od 'to dig, cultivate'

*w

A proto-phoneme *w is set up for the labio-velar glide w corresponding between all Sam
languages.

    R wên 'big (of living beings)' : S wein; weyn : J wîiŋ : B wîi 'big'
    R war'âba M : S waraabe-ha : J waraabâ-gi : B war'âa M 'hyena'
    R ñawâl F : B hawaal F 'grave' : S ñabaal (-she)

*w has become b intervocally in Somali.

*y

A proto-phoneme *y is set up for the palatal glide y corresponding between all Sam languages.

R yañ(a)s'ĭ M : S yeñaas-ki : J yah'āas M 'crocodile'
R yeṟy'êr 'narrow' : S yaṟ 'small, young' : J yeṟ 'small'
R ôy 'to cry' : S oy 'to weep' : B ôy 'to cry'
R gôy : S goy : B kôy 'to cut'

*z

There is a series of correspondences R y : S d : J d : B d for which in accordance with earlier Cushitic reconstructions (see Sasse 1975b: 7ff.) a Proto-Sam phoneme *z is set up.

R s'êyyañ : S sadeñ-di; saddeñ-da : J sĭddĭi : B sĭdde'; sĭddeh 'three'
R gey M : S geid-ki : J geed 'tree' : B k'êed-ka 'this tree'
R yeyañ : S dayañ-a 'moon'
R ñiy M : S ñidid-ki : B h'ĭid M 'root'

It appears that *z got lost in Rendille if preceded and followed by *ĭ:

R miig : S midig-ti : B m'ĭdig 'right (side)'
R rix : S ridiq 'to grind'

*ɔ

There is a series R ñ : S φ (ɔ) : B ɔ which does not occur in morpheme-initial position. Its phonetic equivalent in Proto-Sam is unclear. Hans-Jürgen Sasse (personal communication of 25-7-76) suggests that it goes back to an East Cushitic glottal stop *ɔ. We tentatively assume that this phoneme was represented in Proto-Sam as a glottal stop *ɔ as well, which merged with *h (> ñ) in Rendille.

R riñ'ĭ : S ri-da : J ri' 'goat'
R nañas M : S naas-ka : B n'ā'as M 'female breast'
R guñ : J gūū-ki 'year' : S guu-gi 'long rainy season'
R sañ 'late morning' : S saa-ka 'this morning' : B sa''aa

*ᶜ

The pharyngal plosive ᶜ of Somali corresponds to a pharyngal fricative ñ in Rendille and φ (zero) in Boni in word-initial position. For this series a proto-phoneme *ᶜ is reconstructed.

R ñus'ûb : S ᶜusub 'new' : B 'usub F 'newness'
R ñaan'û M : S ᶜaano-ha : B aanᵉ Pl 'milk'
R ños F 'grass' : S ᶜaws-ka 'dry grass' : B aasᵉ Pl 'grass'

In non-initial position, *ᶜ was replaced by a glottal stop in both Boni and Jabarti, in Jabarti optionally also as h:

R rañ : S raaᶜ : B r'āa' : J ra'; rah 'to follow'
R sañ F : S saᶜ-a : J saa' : B sâ' F 'cow'
R soño : S soᶜo : B sô'o 'to walk, go'
S kaĭ-i : B ka' (ED) : J ka'; kah 'to stand up'

Note that some Rendille speakers have retained ᶜ as a free variant of ñ, e.g. soño or soᶜo 'to walk, go'.

3.1.1.1. Consonant Clusters

Proto-Sam can be assumed to have had a number of consonant clusters of which the most frequent are discussed briefly below. Predominant patterns of clustering are those involving

nasals and liquids as first constituents. Since there are usually only very few examples
for each cluster, in some cases there is only one example, the following reconstructions
have to be considered tentative.

mb

This cluster is set up for Somali and Rendille *mb*, corresponding to *m* in Boni.

   R *cimbir* F : S *shimbir-ta* : B *sh'imir* F 'bird'
   S *ħambaar* 'to carry on back' : *ham'āar* 'to carry'

nd̲

There is a regular correspondence between Rendille and Somali *nd̲* and *n(n)* of Boni for
which a cluster *nd̲* is reconstructed.

   R *mindax'ār* F : S *mind̲iqir-ka* : B *mini²'ir* F (E) 'intestines'
   R *ind̲ô* M : S *indo-ha* : B *inneᵉ* Pl 'eyes'
   R *hand̲'ûr* F : B *han'ûur* F 'navel'
   S *qand̲o-di* 'chills' : B *'ānneᵉ* F 'fever'

ng

ng in Somali and Rendille again corresponds to a simple nasal *n* or *ŋ* in Boni.

   R *'āngag* : S *engeg-an* 'dry' : B *'āneg* M 'dryness'
   S *hunguri-gi* : B *haŋûreᵉ* M (Ed) 'throat'

ng preceding *i* has a considerably divergent series of correspondences (cf. *g), i.e.
R *nj* : S *nj* : B *sh*.

   R *inj'ir* F : S *injir-ta* : B *ishir* F 'louse'

mm

This double consonant is very tentatively set up for a series where Somali has *b* corresponding to *m* (in Jabarti occasionally *mm*) in other Sam languages.

   R *l'āma* : S *laba-di* : J *lāmma* 'two'
   R *tom'ôn* : S *toban-ki* : J *tumôŋ* : B *tamân* 'ten'
   S *kibis-ti* : B *kam'is* (E) 'bread'
   S *dabaalo* : B *duumaal* (Ed) 'to swim'

nk

This reconstruction is based on a correspondence R *nx* : S *nk*. Reflexes in other languages
have not been found.

   R *sonx'ôr* F : S *sonkor-ti* 'sugar'
   R *anx'ād* M 'lightning' : S *onkod-ki* 'thunder'

ns

Somali *ns* seems to correspond to *s* in Boni for which a cluster *ns* is tentatively set up:

   S *qaanso-da* : B *'āāseᵉ* F 'bow'

l + voiceless consonant

It seems that in a number of Proto-Sam words *l* preceded other consonants. In Somali, the
relevant clusters have been retained whereas in Boni *l* has been lost:

R *il'ím*, Pl *ilm'ó* F/M : S *ilmo-di* : B *ilmᵉ* M 'tear' (of eyes)
R *kald'ái*: B *kál'de'da* (E) 'alone'

3.1.2. Vowels

The reconstruction of the Proto-Sam vowel system is a task that, given the limited data available at present, would appear almost impossible to solve. The main problems are: (1) There are inconsistencies in the correspondence of vowels, both with reference to vowel quality and quantity; (2) evidence from Somali suggests that Proto-Sam might have distinguished two sets of five vowels each, with the distinction being based on either laxness vs. tenseness or on the position of the tongue root; yet the data from other Sam languages do not quite seem to support such a reconstruction.

The following attempt at reconstructing Proto-Sam vowels must therefore be considered very tentative only. It is to be hoped that it will help to stimulate more detailed research in the field.

Underlying our reconstructions are some tentative assumptions on Sam vowel change patterns, the most important of which are:

(i) The history of Somali is characterized by the introduction of a progressive assimilation rule

$$V_1 - X - V_2 \rightarrow V_1 - X - V_1 \text{ (where X = any consonant)}$$

(ii) Rendille and Boni, on the other hand, have an opposite, regressive, assimilation rule of the kind

$$V_1 - X - V_2 \rightarrow V_2 - X - V_2$$

This rule appears to have been introduced in Rendille earlier than in Boni.

(iii) Boni has a lip-rounding rule

$$\begin{bmatrix} +\text{vocalic} \\ -\text{conson.} \end{bmatrix} \rightarrow \begin{bmatrix} -\text{low} \\ +\text{back} \end{bmatrix} \quad / \underline{\quad} b$$

not shared by other Sam languages.

*a

All languages have a vowel *a* corresponding regularly with each other. For this series, a proto-phoneme **a* is set up.

   R *fár* M : S *far-ta* : J *far* : B *far* F 'finger'
   R *cán* F : S *shan-ta* : J *shaŋ* : B *shâŋ* 'five'
   F *'áfar* : S *afar-ta* : J *áfar* : B *áfar* 'four'

There are several other series which can be said to go back to Proto-Sam **a*. These series have in common that Somali *a* corresponds to vowels other than *a* in Rendille and Boni:

S *a* : R *o* : B *o*

   R *somb'ób* M : S *sambab-ka* : B *somb'óbᵉ* M 'lungs'
   R *dow'óño* F : S *dawaᶜo-di* 'jackal'
   S *maroodi-gi* : B *mor'óórᵉ* F 'elephant'

S *a* : R *i* : B *i*

   R *sir'ír* F : S *sariir-ta* : B *sir'íir* F 'bed'
   R *mind'íla* F 'shaving knife' : S *mandiil (-sha)* : B *mînnᵉ* (E) 'knife'
   R *fíddiso* (Fleming 1964:70) : S *faddiso* : B *f'íriiso* 'to sit'

It is assumed that both Rendille and Boni have assimilated *a regressively to the following vowel.

There are, however, examples where this assimilation has taken place in Rendille though not in Boni:

R ñol'ŏŏlo F 'stomach' : S ᶜalool-shi 'belly' : B al'ŏol M 'stomach'
R xob'ŏb F 'cold (n)' : S qaboob-hi 'cold weather' : B ab'ŏob M 'coolness'

Neither in Rendille nor in Boni is the assimilation rule applied across morpheme boundaries.

Together with the regressive assimilation of Rendille and Boni, a progressive assimilation a → e / e (X) __ may have occurred in Somali, as the following examples suggest:

R ḍ'ǎrag 'to be satisfied' : S ḍereg : B 'd'ěrek 'to be satiated'
R gàs F : S gees-ka 'horn' : B k'ǎas M 'molar'

Another series R a : S a : B u/o can equally be said to be derived from *a. The Boni reflexes are due to the lip-rounding rule mentioned above.

R g'ǎrab M 'shoulderblade' : S qarab-ka : B k'ǎrub M 'shoulder'
S ᶜarrab-ki : B 'ǎrub M 'tongue'
R dab M : S dab-ka : B tŏb M 'fire'
R x'ǎbo : S qabo : B 'ŏbo 'to catch, seize, hold'

Short *a frequently corresponds to i in Jabarti (cf. von Tiling 1922:32), occasionally also in Boni:

R matañ M : S madañ-a : J mǎdi' : B m'ǎda' M 'head'
S shabeel-ka : J shiβěěl : B shub'ěel M 'leopard'
R 'ǎḍi M : S aḍi-gi : J iṛi : B 'iṛᵉ M 'sheep and goats'

*e

All Sam languages have a corresponding series of e for which a proto-phoneme *e is set up.

R hel : S hel : B hel 'to get'
R dèr : S der 'long, tall' : J deer 'high' : B 'd'ěer 'long, tall'
R meel F : S meel (-sha) : B meel F 'place'

*i

This Proto-Sam phoneme is reconstructed on the basis of a series of i in all languages.

R il F : S il (-sha) : J il : B ǐl F 'eye'
R min M : J miŋ : B mǐŋ M 'house'
R s'ii : S sii : B sǐi 'to give'
R bûñi : S buuñi : B b'ûûñi 'to fill'

In some cases, the reflex of Boni is e rather than i:

S tiri : B t'ěrᵉ 'to count'
R ñiḍ : S ñid : B hir, hêr 'to close, shut, tie'

There is a series R a : S a : B i for which a Proto-Sam segment *ai is tentatively set up.

R gas'ǎr M : B k'ǐsᵉ F 'buffalo'
S gaḍ-ka : B kǐr M 'chin'
R gǎn : B kǐn 'to shoot'

Note that in all cases involved the consonant preceding *ai is *g.

The lip-rounding rule applying to vowels preceding b in Boni (see above) is also relevant to vowels derived from *i:

R j'ilib M : S jilib-ka : B sh'ilub M 'knee' (but: B shilibtǎa Pl 'knees')

*o

All Sam languages have a corresponding series of *o* for which a proto-phoneme **o* is set up.

   R *tôl* : S *tol* : B *tol* 'to sew'
   R *gôy* : S *goy* : B *kôy* 'to cut'
   R *kôw* : S *kow-da* : J *kow; koo* : B *kôw* 'one'

In a number of examples, Rendille, Jabarti and Boni *o* corresponds to *a* in Somali:

   R *kob* F : S *kab-ti* : B *kôb* F 'shoe, sandal'
   R *môg* F 'debt' : S *mag-ti* 'blood money'
   R *ico* : S *iyâ-ga* : J *iyyoo* : B *iyo* 'they'

*u

All Sam languages have a vowel *u* regularly corresponding with each other.

   R *kuß* : S *kuß* : B *kûß* 'to fall'
   R *nûg* : S *nuug* : B *n'ûug* 'to suck (from breast)'
   R *ħus'ûb* : S *ᶜusub* 'new' : B *'usub* F 'newness'

3.1.2.1. Vowel Clusters

Proto-Sam must have had a number of vowel combinations that may have formed rising diphthongs. These combinations have been retained in Somali but were usually replaced by single short or long vowels in the other Sam languages.

   R *ħoß* F 'grass' : S *ᶜaws-ka* 'dry grass' : B *aas^e* Pl 'grass'
   R *ôr* M 'bull (camel)' : S *awr-ka* 'burden camel' : B *ôor* M 'male elephant'
   R *cel'ê* : S *shalei; sheley* : B *shâl^e* (E) 'yesterday'
   R *kul'êl* M : S *kulayl-ka; kuleil-ki* : B *kul'êel* M 'heat'
   R *wên* 'big (of living beings)' : S *wein; weyn* : J *wiiŋ* : B *wii/wiin-* 'big'

3.1.2.2. The Semi-mute Vowel of Boni

There is a set of largely devoiced centralized vowels [ɤ̣], [ụ̈], and [ɔ̣] which appear to be variants of one vowel phoneme *^e*. This phoneme corresponds to short vowels both in the other Sam languages and in Proto-Sam. From the data available it is not possible to establish what phonetic equivalent of this vowel there was in Proto-Sam. Further research on this problem is urgently required.

Proto-Sam

*a	R *gas'âr* M : B *k'is^e* F 'buffalo'
*e	S *wadne-ha* : B *w'ênd^e* F 'heart'
*i	R *k'âri* : S *kari* : B *k'âr^e* 'to cook, boil'
*o	R *farr'ô* M : S *faro* : B *far^e* Pl 'fingers'
*u	R *ħaan'û* M : S *ᶜaano-ha* : B *aan^e* Pl 'milk'

3.1.3. The Proto-Sam System

The above reconstructions suggest that the hypothetical ancestor language of the present-day spoken Sam languages had the following phonemes:

3.1.3.1. Consonants

	Bilab.	Lab.-dent.	Dent.	Alv.	Post-alv.	Pal.	Vel.	Uvul.	Glott.	Phar.
Plosive			*t			*c	*k	*q	*ʔ	*ʕ
	*b		*d		*ḍ	*g				
Fricative		*ɓ	*s						*h	*ħ
			*z							
Lateral			*l							
Roll			*r							
Nasal	*m		*n							
Glide	*w					*y				

Most of these consonants occurred both as single as well as double consonants (cf. Comp. Voc., Ch. 6). In addition, Proto-Sam must have distinguished various consonant clusters of which the most conspicuous have been mentioned above (3.1.1).

The following distributional characteristics of individual consonants may be noted:

(1) *g has the alternant *[dʒ] preceding high front vowels.

(2) *b is likely to be pronounced *[β] in intervocalic position.

3.1.3.2. Vowels

Proto-Sam had a least the following five vowels:

*i   *u

    *e   *o

        *a

These vowels occur both as short (*a, *e, etc.) and as long vowels (*aa, *ee, *ii, *oo, *uu). Whether there was a third category of vowels, as the semi-mute vowels of Boni suggest, remains to be investigated.

Another problem that needs further investigation is whether Proto-Sam may not have distinguished two sets of vowels based on the distinction of tenseness and/or tongue root positions.

3.1.3.3. Tone and Accent

A systematic comparative treatment of tone and accent in the Sam languages has not yet been attempted. From our survey, however, it would seem that some tentative generalisations are possible:

(1) It is likely that Proto-Sam was a tone language distinguishing between High (á), Low (à)[14] and High-falling tone (â).

---

[14]Note that in this paper Low tone is unmarked in actually spoken language data. In reconstructed morphemes, Low is consistently marked by an *accent grave* (see 3.0, Table 1).

(2) One of the functions of tone was to distinguish sex gender of nouns denoting human beings or animals. Thus, it is possible to reconstruct word pairs like *'ínàm M 'boy' : *ìn'ăm F 'girl' , *q'áâℓìm M 'young male camel' : *qâāℓ'ìm F 'young female camel', or *w'áĥàɾ M 'male kid' : *wàĥ'àɾ F 'female kid' which are distinguished by tone only (but see (3)). Note that in each case the tone pattern is High-Low with Masculine and Low-High with Feminine nouns (cf. 3.3.2).

(3) In addition to three tones (see (1)), Proto-Sam can be assumed to have marked an accent which in most, though not all, cases coincides with High tone. Whether the accent ('a) had distinctive function remains to be investigated.

3.2. WORD ORDER

The basic word order of all modern Sam languages is very much alike and it would seem that the past development of these languages was marked by very few changes only.

Proto-Sam can be described as a language belonging to the GALLA sub-type of type D (see Heine 1976d), i.e. it can be assumed to have been characterized by the following order of constituents:

(1) The order of basic sentence constituents is Subject-Object-Verb. This order is found in all Sam languages, e.g.

R maxabaℓ w'ěℓ-e ĵ'ěĥ-e (man child hit)	'The man hit the child.'	
B 'děěk-a ôy k'ĩ-'diɣit-a (child dog hits)	'The child hits the dog.'	
J 'ăni seeɣ mö-qôb-o (I sword not-have)	'I have no sword.' (von Tiling 1921/22:149)	
S geeℓ baɾiis ma ʿun-o (camels rice not eat)	'Camels don't eat rice.' (Bell 1953:66)	

(2) The adverbial phrase likewise precedes the verb (see 3.4).

(3) The auxiliary follows the main verb.

(4) Interrogative words usually precede the verb.

(5) Postpositions, rather than prepositions, are used (see 3.4).

(6) The genitive follows its governing noun (see 3.3.3.4).

(7) Nominal determiners and qualifiers follow the noun (see 3.3.3), with the exception of the numeral which precedes (see 3.3.3.2).

(8) The bound object pronoun precedes the verb (see 3.5.3.1), but the bound subject pronouns follow it (3.6.4.1) with one exception (3.6.4.2).

(9) Tense/aspect markers usually follow the verb.

(10) The negative marker either precedes or both precedes and follows the verb (3.6.4).

The only notable change of word order that seems to have occurred in the development of the Sam languages was the placement of the numeral from its pre-nominal to a post-nominal position in Rendille (see 3.3.3.2).

3.3. NOUN PHRASE

3.3.1. Number

Nominal number distinctions in Proto-Sam are expressed by means of suffixes. There are at least two basic categories on nouns (cf. 3.3.2), i.e. (1) those forming their plural by means of a suffix *-o, and (2) those that reduplicate the last syllable of the noun in order to derive the plural from the singular.

The majority of nouns belong to (1). With a few exceptions (see below), their gender is Feminine in singular and Masculine in plural:

    *aḍañ, Pl *aḍañ-o F/M 'back'
    *arit, Pl *arit-o F/M 'gate of animal pan'
    *bèèr, Pl *bèèr-o F/M 'garden'
    *cimbir, Pl *cimbir-o F/M 'bird'
    *ḍeg, Pl *ḍeg-o F/M 'ear'
    *far, Pl *far-o F/M 'finger'
    *galeb, Pl *galeb-o F/M 'evening'
    *ilm, Pl *ilm-'ô F/M 'tear (of eye)'
    *kob, Pl *kob-o F/M 'shoe, sandal'
    *kor, Pl kor-o F/M 'camel-bell'
    *laf, Pl *laf-o F/M 'bone'
    *la'am, Pl *la'am-o F/M 'branch'
    *sariir, Pl *sariir-o F/M 'bed'
    *ul, Pl *ul-o F/M 'stick'
    *ᶜal'ool, Pl *ᶜalool-o F/M 'stomach'

A smaller number of nouns are Masculine in both singular and plural:

    *g'ilib, Pl *gilb-'ô M/M 'knee'
    *g'àràb, Pl *garb-o M/M 'shoulderblade'
    *geiz, Pl *geiz-'ô M/M 'tree'
    *na'as, Pl *na'as-o M/M 'female breast'

Nouns ending in *-i have *-yo instead of *-o as their plural suffix:

    *cinni, Pl cinni-yo F/M 'bed'
    *rimai, Pl rimai-yo 'uterus, womb of animals'

Nouns belonging to (2) are monosyllabic and Masculine in gender in both singular and plural. The vowel of the reduplicated syllable is a throughout:

    *dab, Pl *dab-ab M/M 'fire'
    *diim, Pl *diim-am M/M 'tortoise'
    *gog, Pl *gog-ag M/M 'skin of persons and camels'
    *sam, Pl *sam-am M/M 'nose'
    *ur, Pl *ur-ar M/M 'belly, abdomen'
    *weil, Pl *wèil-'àl M 'child'
    *ᶜoz, Pl *ᶜoz-az M/M 'voice'

Apart from these two predominant categories, Proto-Sam probably had various other, less common, patterns of nominal number treatment:

(3) In a few cases, number was distinguished by means of suppletive stems:

*il, Pl *indo F/M 'eye'
*in'ám, Pl *ʾalb- F/M 'girl, daughter'
*saᶜ, Pl *loiʾ F/F 'cow'

(4) Some nouns seem to have expressed number distinctions by a change of gender only, e.g. *dagañ, Pl *dagañ M/F 'stone'.

(5) Other nouns again probably had no number distinction at all, e.g.

*ḍiig M 'blood'   *soor F 'food'
*hafar M 'wind'   *subañ M 'butter'
*roob M 'rain'   *ᶜaanu M 'milk'
*sonkor F 'sugar'

More recent research on Rendille by Oomen (1977a) seems to indicate that there may have been a noun class which was Masculine in singular and Feminine in plural. This class, which is likely to have been different from class (4), might have been as common as class (1). More research is needed on this question.

3.3.2. Gender

Proto-Sam is a gender language having the following characteristics:

(1) There are two grammatical genders, Masculine and Feminine, Masculine being the unmarked one.

(2) The singular and plural forms of a given noun may be the same gender (see 3.3.1 (2)) — but with the majority of nouns there might have been a system of POLARITY where by a Masculine singular noun is Feminine in plural and vice versa, i.e. Feminine singular nouns having Masculine plural forms (but see below).

(3) A change in gender may be the only means of distinguishing singular and plural of certain nouns (3.3.1).

(4) There is some correlation between sex and grammatical gender in nouns denoting human beings and animals: the singular of nouns denoting males is usually constructed with the Masculine gender and the singular of females with the Feminine gender. In addition, differences in sex are expressed by means of tonal oppositions in that nouns denoting males have the tone pattern High-Low, nouns denoting female concepts having the opposite contour Low-High (see 3.1.3).

(5) There is grammatical agreement between the gender of a noun and certain grammatical categories governed by the latter. Such categories are demonstrative, possessive and personal pronouns.

Looking at the gender/number distinction of reconstructed Proto-Sam nouns one remarkable observation can be made: apart from very few exceptions, the plural of nouns is generally of the Masculine gender, distinctions in gender thus being confined to the singular. This situation resembles that found in Boni and differs remarkably from that of Rendille and Somali which use both genders in the plural to more or less the same extent. Although there can be hardly any doubt that Proto-Sam used both genders in the plural, it would seem that this hypothetical language has many traces of an earlier system in which gender distinctions were neutralized in the plural, Masculine being the unmarked gender used for both genders.

3.3.3. Dependent Categories

3.3.3.1. Adjectives

The Proto Sam adjective can be assumed to have had the following characteristics:

(1) It follows the noun it qualifies;

(2) with some possible exceptions, it does not show any gender agreement with the governing noun, although there was probably a gender-sensitive particle linking the two;

(3) its plural form is derived from the singular by reduplicating the first syllable or segment.

Adjectives reconstructable for Proto-Sam are:

*wein, Pl *wa-wein 'big, large'
*ɗèèr, Pl *ɗèr-ɗèèr 'long, tall'
*yer, Pl *yer-yer 'small'
*ᶜusub, Pl *ᶜus-ᶜusub 'new'
*ᶜuľ'ês, Pl *ᶜuľ-ᶜuľes 'heavy'
*ᶜaidi, Pl *ᶜaid-ᶜaidi 'unripe'
*qaboo, Pl *qab-qaboo 'cold'
*ħum, Pl *ħum-ħum 'bad'

Proto-Sam is likely to have had only a very restricted set of genuine adjectives.

3.3.3.2. Numerals

The numeral system of Proto-Sam is decimal, the following numerals having been reconstructed:

*kôw	1	*liħ	6
*lámma	2	*tVzzoba[15]	7
*sízzaħ	3	*sìzy'èèt	8
*'áƒàr	4	*saagal	9
*can	5	*tomm'an	10

Combinations of tens and digits are formed by placing *iccou between *tomm'an and the following numeral:

*tomm'an iccou kôw	'11 (10 + 1)'
*tomm'an iccou lámma	'12 (10 + 2)'

The attributive use of Proto-Sam numerals can be characterized thus:

(1) The numeral precedes the noun it qualifies. The only modern Sam language deviating from this pattern is Rendille which places the numeral after the noun. In Somali, Jabarti and Boni the numeral precedes the noun although in those areas of Boni country where Swahili is used as a second language the numeral tends to follow the noun (see Heine 1977:25).

(2) There is no gender agreement between numeral and noun.

---

[15]The symbol 'V' stands for a vowel whose quality we have not yet been able to determine.

(3) Nouns denoting non-human concepts are used in the singular when qualified by numerals,[16] e.g.

*'áɓáʀ geiz	'four trees'
*tomm'an ɓaʀ	'ten fingers'

(4) Evidence from Eastern Sam as well as from Eastern Cushitic languages outside Sam suggests that tens are formed by combining digits with the root *-tom, which is a shortened form of *tomm'an 'ten'. The following tens can be tentatively reconstructed.

*lámma-tom	'20'
*sózz-om (< *sízz-tom)	'30'
*'áɓaʀ-tom	'40'
*liñ-tom	'60'
*tVzzoba-tom	'70'
*sízy'êèt-tom	'80'
*saagas-som, *saagal-tom	'90'

3.3.3.3. Demonstratives

Proto-Sam must have had a detailed deictic system of spatial and temporal reference. From the evidence available it seems that at least five demonstrative categories were distinguished (cf. Andrzejewski 1964:119):

I	[+ NEAR]	*-an	'this, these'
II	[- FAR]	*-a	'this, these (there)'
III	[- NEAR]	*-aas	'that, those'
IV	[+ FAR]	*-oo	'that, those (there)'
V	[+ PAST]	*-ii	'that, those (referred to earlier)'

These demonstrative morphemes are preceded by the gender markers *k for M(asculine) and *t for F(eminine) which agree with the governing noun. The resulting forms are thus:

	M	F
I	*k-an	*t-an
II	*k-a	*t-a
III	*k-aas	*t-aas
IV	*k-oo	*t-oo
V	*k-ii	*t-ii

The demonstratives follow the noun they determine, e.g.

*cimbiʀ t-an, Pl *cimbiʀ-o k-an 'this bird'
*geiz k-aas, Pl *geiz-'ó k-aas 'that tree'
*ʀoob k-a 'this rain'
*sooʀ t-a 'this food'
*ᶜaanu k-ii 'that milk (referred to earlier)'
*bèèʀ t-oo 'that garden (far away)'

The function of these demonstratives has changed in various ways in the modern Sam languages. These changes are summarized in Table 2.

---

[16]It may be that originally only Masculine nouns occurred without plural endings when preceded by a numeral whereas Feminine nouns used a suffix *-ood, which has been retained in Jabarti and Somali, e.g. J síddii láŋ 'three men' but ᵓáɓaʀ habʀ-óód 'four women'.

Thus, it would seem that Rendille lost IV *-oo but acquired a new demonstrative -'us 'that (middle distance)'. Boni appears to have lost both I *-an and III *-aas. In Jabarti, II *-a and I *-an have merged into -e-áŋ whereas IV *-oo and V *-ii seem to have disappeared from the language. In Somali, all Proto-Sam demonstratives have been retained formally but II *-a and V *-ii have become Deictic Determiners ("definite article"; see Tucker/Bryan 1966:525). In addition, there is a demonstrative -eer in Somali which cannot be traced back to Proto-Sam.

TABLE 2
DEVELOPMENT OF PROTO-SAM DEMONSTRATIVES

---

[17]The connector -i of Rendille links the noun with its dependent categories such as adjectives, (genitive) noun phrases, and relative clauses.

There is no clear evidence suggesting that Proto-Sam had any determinative form that could be labelled "Deictic Determiner" or "definite article". Somali seems to be the only Sam language that has Deictic Determiners, both being derived from demonstratives.

3.3.3.4. Nominal Possessives

The nominal possessive (genitive) of Proto-Sam is formed by simply placing the *nomen rectum* after the *nomen regens*. This pattern occurs in all Sam languages with the exception of Rendille which places a gender-sensitive connector (*kí/kíye* for M and *tí/tíye* for F) between the two noun phrases.[18] In Somali, the *nomen rectum* is usually required in the definite form, i.e. it is followed by the *-a* ending definite suffixes[19] (see Kirk 1905:26).

Masculine and Feminine genitives can be assumed to have differed in their inflexional behaviour: whereas a Masculine *nomen rectum* has no case ending, a Feminine *nomen rectum*, i.e. most of those nouns that form their plural by suffixing *-o (see 3.3.1), would take the case suffixes *-eet in singular and *-ot in plural.

Examples of reconstructed possessive constructions are:

indo weil	'the eyes of a child' ('child eyes')
kūl'āīl dab-ab	'the heat of fires'
bice(o) lañas	'water of the well'

but

laƒ-o cimbir-eet	'bones of a bird' ('bone-Pl bird-of')
laƒ-o cimbir-o-ot	'bones of birds' (bone-Pl bird-Pl-of')
ᶜoz cinni-eet	'the voice of a bee'
ᶜoz cinni-yo-ot	'the voice of bees'

For the pronominal possessive see 3.5.2.

3.4. ADVERBIAL PHRASE

The adverbial phrase of Proto-Sam follows both the subject and the object nouns but precedes the verb. It consists either of a combination of noun + postposition or of an adverb.

Postpositions are mostly derived from noun phrases, i.e. combinations consisting of a noun followed by a pronominal possessive, e.g.

min hor-t-iis	'in front of the house' ('house front-its')

---

[18]This gender particle is derived from the Proto-Sam reference demonstrative V *k-íi M, *t-íi F; see 3.3.3.3).

[19]Somali has an alternative order *rectum - regens* where the *nomen regens* is qualified by a possessive pronoun:

awr alaab-tiis	'the loads of a camel' (Bell 1953:70)
camel loads-his	

3.5. PERSONAL PRONOUNS

3.5.1. Independent Pronouns

The independent pronouns of Proto-Sam are (cf. Comp. Voc.; Ch. 6):

Sg 1	*aní	Pl 1 Incl.	*inno
2	*atí	2	*atín
3 M	*usu	3	*ico
F	*íce		

There can be hardly any doubt that Proto-Sam had a distinction Inclusive/Exclusive in independent pronouns. The exact shape of the Pl 1 Exclusive pronoun (R *nañ*, S *anna-gu*), however, has not yet been reconstructed.

The singular pronouns of Proto-Sam are likely to have had alternative forms without final vowels, i.e.

Sg 1	*an
2	*at
3 M	*us
F	*ic

These forms are attested in all Sam languages.

3.5.2. Possessive Pronouns

Possessive pronouns follow the noun they qualify and agree with it in gender. The gender prefix is *k* for Masculine and *t* for Feminine pronouns. The various pronouns are:

Sg 1	*-ay	Pl 1 Incl.	*-eena
2	*-aña	2	*-iin
3 M	*-iis	3	*-ood
F	*-eed		

A distinction Inclusive/Exclusive probably existed but, in the same way as with the independent pronouns, no form of the Exclusive pronoun can be reconstructed.

The possessive pronouns of Proto-Sam are most fully retained in Boni, whereas both Jabarti and Somali use shortened forms. Rendille has added a final *a* and, in the case of the 3rd person pronouns, prefixed the independent pronouns:

		R	B	S	J
Sg 1		-aya	-e	-ay	-ee
2		-aña	-aha	-aa	-aa
3 M		-isa	-is	-iis	-yee, -iis
F		-ice-eda	-ee'e	-eed	-(iy)ye
Pl 1	Incl.	-eena	-ani	-eena	-aanu
	Excl.	-anya		-yo	
2		-iina	-eni	-iina	-iiŋ
3		-ico-oda	-oo'd	-oo, -ood	-yoo

3.5.3. VERBAL PRONOUNS

3.5.3.1. Object Pronouns

Independent pronouns are used both as subject and object pronouns. For the Sg 1 and Sg 2, Proto-Sam has obligatory object pronouns in addition. They immediately precede the verb root. These prefixes are *i- (Sg 1) and *ku-/*ki- (Sg 2). Sg 2 prefixes *ku- and *ki- are likely to have co-existed as optional variants in Proto-Sam. *ki- occurs in Rendille and Jabarti whereas Somali and Boni use *ku-.

Furthermore, all Eastern Sam languages, but not Rendille, have a Pl 1 object prefix. The shape of this prefix differs from language to language (B nu-, J ni-, S na-, ina-). On the basis of the evidence available it does not seem possible to decide whether Proto-Sam had a Pl 1 object pronoun.

3.5.3.2. Subject Pronouns

Proto-Sam has both subject prefixes and suffixes. The former are used with a minority of verbs usually referred to as Prefix-Verbs ("strong verbs"; see 3.6.4.2). All other verbs, i.e. the Suffix-Verbs ("weak verbs"; see 3.6.4.1), take suffixes only. The phonological shape of both affix series is basically the same, with the exception of the 3rd person:

		Prefix pronouns	Suffix pronouns
Sg 1		*ϕ-, *y-	*ϕ
2		*t-	*$-t$
3 M		*y-	*ϕ
F		*t-	*$-t$
Pl 1		*n-	*$-n$
2		*t- ... -Vn	*$-tVn$
3		*y- ... -Vn	*$-Vn$

The symbol "V" in the Pl 2 and Pl 3) stands for a vowel whose quality depends on both aspect and conjugation type (see 3.6.4).

Each phonological constituent has a clearly defined function:

*ϕ	=	Sg 1, Sg 3 M (except Prefix pronouns)
*t	=	2 or F
*n	=	Pl 1
*V	=	Pl 2, Pl 3
*y	=	3 M (Prefix pronouns only)

The Suffix pronouns (except Pl 2 and Pl 3 are followed by an obligatory vowel marking aspect/mood (see 3.6.3).

Although the Sg 1 and Sg 3 M, as well as Sg 2 and Sg 3 F pronouns, respectively, are usually formally identical, there are a few verbs that distinguish between them. The verb "to go", for example, has the following singular forms in Rendille and Boni:

		R	B	
Sg 1		'ird-a	á-d'ed-a	'I go, shall go'
2		'ira-ta	á-d'e-ta	
3 M		'irt-a	á-d'ed-a	
F		'ire-ta	á-d'e-ta	

The subject pronouns of Proto-Sam do not distinguish between Pl 1 Inclusive and Exclusive pronouns.

3.6. VERB

The verb root is usually monosyllabic and has the structure *CV(V)C in the vast majority of cases, e.g.

*ɓîl	'to comb'	*tuus	'to show'
*gut	'to circumcise'	*yeel	'to do'
*hèl	'to get'		
*ħat	'to steal'		

3.6.1. Imperative

The Imperative consists of the simple verb stem. It has either Low or High-falling tone with monosyllabic roots and usually the pattern High - Low with bisyllabic roots. The Pl 2 Imperative is formed by adding the suffix *-à to the singular Imperative. The syllable preceding this suffix gets both High tone and accent:

*arg, Pl *'árg-à		'see!'
*dûr, Pl *d'úr-à		'play, sing!'
*ɗís, Pl *ɗ'ís-à		'build!'
*gal, Pl *g'ál-à		'enter!'
*giit, Pl *g'íit-à		'pull!'
*waᶜ, Pl *w'áᶜ-à		'call!'
*ħaw'áàl, Pl *ħàw'áál-à		'bury!'
*k'áálèî, Pl *kàál'éí-à		'come!'
*kor, Pl *k'ór-à		'climb!'
*raaᶜ, Pl *r'ááᶜ-à		'follow!'
*làb, Pl *l'áb-à		'return it!'
*tum, Pl *t'úm-à		'pound!'

The plural suffix is *-cà for verbs having the Causative ending *-î (see 3.6.5.2.2) and *-dà for verbs ending in *-ò (Reflexive; see 3.6.5.2.1), e.g.

*búúħ-î, Pl *bùùħ-'î-cà	'fill!'
*k'íᶜî, Pl *k'íᶜî-cà	'wake up!'
*neeɓ-s-o, Pl *neeɓ-sî-ɗà	'breathe!'
*d'éᶜ-ò, Pl *dêᶜò-ɗà	'belch!'

3.6.2. Infinitive

Proto-Sam may have had a suffix *-an expressing both infinitive and participial functions, e.g.

*keen-an	'to bring, brought'
*k'ár-î-an	'to cook, cooked'
*waᶜ-an	'to call, called'

This suffix is retained in Rendille as an infinitive marker -'án, in Somali as a Static suffix -an (Bell 1953:114) and in Jabarti as a participle -aŋ, "which has a passive meaning" (von Tiling 1921/22:143).

Boni has an infinitive suffix -'ó which is likely to have the same origin as the infinitive suffix *-oow* (*-oo*, *-aaw*) of Jabarti (von Tiling 1921/22:138-142). Whether these suffixes go back to an infinitive form of the Proto-Sam verb remains to be investigated.

3.6.3. Aspect

Proto-Sam does not seem to have distinguished "genuine" verb tenses, deictic time being expressed by means of temporal adverbs like *máän-tã* 'today', *celei* 'yesterday', etc. which precede the verb.

However, there must have been an aspectual distinction Imperfect/Perfect which correlates strongly with deictic time: the Imperfect has the semantic feature [-PAST], i.e. it usually expresses verbal actions in either the present or the future, whereas the Perfect has the feature [+PAST] and typically indicates actions in the past.

The following shapes of the aspect markers of Suffix-Verbs (see 3.6.4.1) can be reconstructed:

Imperfect:	*-a*,	Pl 2,3:	*-aan*
Perfect:	*-ay*,	Pl 2,3:	*-een*

Modern reflexes of these forms are:

	R	B	S
Imperfect:	*-a*, *-an*	*-a*, *-i*	*-a*, *-aan*
Perfect:	*-e*, *-en*	*-e*, *-e*	*-ay*, *-een*

The Pl 2 and Pl 3 suffix *-i* of the Imperfect in Boni is derived from the Prefix-Verb conjugation, where the Proto-Sam suffix is *-in* (see 3.6.4.2).

Jabarti has retained the Proto-Sam aspect markers as well but here they have merged with the Durative suffix *-ay*,[20] which is also found in Somali but may not have been part of Proto-Sam.

In Prefix-Verbs (see 3.6.4.2), the pattern of aspect distinction is remarkably different: Imperfect and Perfect are distinguished by means of a change in the root vowels. These are either LOW (*a*) or HIGH vowels (*i*, *u*). The combinations occurring and their aspectual significance are:

Imperfect:	*Low - *High,	Pl 2,3:	*Low - *Long High
Perfect:	*High - *High,	Pl 2,3:	*High - *Long Low (cf. Hetzron forthcoming:3.2.3.4)
Negative Perfect:	*High - *(Long) Low		

For examples see 3.6.4.2.

This pattern has been retained in Rendille but has been simplified in all other Sam languages. Jabarti has only very few traces of it left (see 4.1).

No systematic reconstructions have been made for the Subjunctive, but the following tentative remark may be made: for Suffix-Verbs the Proto-Sam Subjunctive is likely to have been marked by a suffix *-o*, Pl 2,3: *-aan*. For Prefix-Verbs, on the other hand, the Subjunctive appears to have been derived from the Perfect forms (*High - *High, Pl 2,3: *High - *Long Low) although there may have been some morphophonological irregularities involved.

---

[20]For a detailed discussion of the development in Jabarti, see von Tiling (1921/22:130-33).

3.6.4. Conjugation Patterns

The finite verbal of Proto-Sam usually has the following structure:

$$*\begin{pmatrix} \text{INDEPENDENT} \\ \text{PRONOUN} \end{pmatrix} \quad \text{(NEG)} \; + \; \begin{matrix} \text{VERB} \\ \text{STEM} \end{matrix} \; + \; \begin{matrix} \text{VERBAL} \\ \text{PRONOUN} \end{matrix} \; + \quad \text{ASPECT}$$

This is the structure of Suffix-Verbs which account for the vast majority of Proto-Sam verbs. Prefix-Verbs place the verbal pronoun before the verb and express aspect by means of ablaut (see 3.6.3).

The independent pronoun is used either to emphasize the noun phrase it represents, or to dis-ambiguate finite forms which are not distinguished formally by bound verbal pronouns. Thus, e.g. a form like *arg-t-ay* may mean either 'you saw' or 'she saw', whereas *ati arg-t-ay* means 'YOU saw' and *ice arg-t-ay* means 'SHE saw' (see 3.5.1).

3.6.4.1. Suffix Verbs

The following person-aspect endings can be reconstructed for Suffix-Verbs ("weak verbs") (cf. 3.5.3.2; 3.6.3):

			Imperfect	Perfect
Sg	1		*-a	*-ay
	2		*-t-a	*-t-ay
	3	M	*-a	*-ay
		F	*-t-a	*-t-ay
Pl	1		*-n-a	*-n-ay
	2		*-t-aa-n	*-t-ee-n
	3		*-aa-n	*-ee-n

The corresponding negative paradigms are:

			Imperfect		Perfect	
Sg	1		*má-	-o	*ani má-	-nin
	2		*má-	-t-o	*ati má-	-nin
	3	M	*má-	-o	*usu má-	-nin
		F	*má-	-t-o	*ice má-	-nin
Pl	1		*má-	-n-o	*inno má-	-nin
	2		*má-	-t-aa-n	*atin má-	-nin
	3		*má-	-aa-n	*ico má-	-nin

The person-aspect suffixes of the negative Imperfect are identical with those of the Subjunctive.

The negative Perfect has an invariable suffix. Distinctions of person are, if needed, expressed by means of isolated pronouns.

3.6.4.2. Prefix-Verbs

Prefix-Verbs ("strong verbs") form a minority of the Proto-Sam verbs. Proto-Sam must have had at least ten of them, but probably their number was considerable higher. All reconstructable Prefix-Verbs belong to the basic vocabulary and can be assumed to be remnants of a formerly much larger set of East Cushitic verbs of this type.

Depending on their root vowel, three classes of Prefix-Verbs have to be distinguished: *-a-verbs, *u-verbs and *i-verbs, although *a-verbs may also be considered a sub-class of *u-verbs. These verbs have *a, *u, and *i, respectively, as their second root vowel in the Imperative.

The following is an attempt at reconstructing the conjugation patters of three representative Proto-Sam verbs. Since Rendille appears to be the only language that has retained the "original" patterns, reconstruction is biased in favor of this language, in some cases to the extent that actually spoken Rendille forms are taken to reflect forms of the proto-language. Concerning the shape of the personal pronouns, see 3.5.3.2, concerning the aspect distinctions, see 3.6.3.

(1)   *a-verbs: *aħam 'to eat'

		Imperfect		Perfect	
Sg	1	*aħam	'I eat, shall eat'	*uħum	'I ate, have eaten'
	2	*t-aħam		*t-uħum	
	3 M	*y-aħam		*y-uħum	
	F	*t-aħam		*t-uħum	
Pl	1	*n-aħam		*n-uħum	
	2	*t-aħam-in		*t-uħum-en	
	3	*y-aħam-in		*y-uħum-en	

		Negative Imperfect		Negative Perfect	
Sg	1	*mā-aħam	'I do not,	*ani mā-uħam-nan	'I did not eat,
	2	*mā-t-aħam	shall not eat'	*ati mā-uħam-nan	have not eaten'
	3 M	*mā-y-aħam		etc.	
	F	*mā-t-aħam			
Pl	1	*mā-n-aħam			
	2	*mā-t-aħam-in			
	3	*mā-y-aħam-in			

(2)   *u-verbs: *amut 'to die'

		Imperfect		Perfect	
Sg	1	*y-amut	'I die, shall die'	*y-umu-i	'I died, have died'
	2	*t-amut		*t-umu-i	
	3 M	*y-amut		*y-umu-i	
	F	*t-amut		*t-umu-i	
Pl	1	*n-amut		*n-umu-i	
	2	*t-amuut-in		*t-umaat-en	
	3	*y-amuut-in		*y-umaat-en	

		Negative Imperfect		Negative Perfect	
Sg	1	*mā-y-amut	'I do not, shall not die'	*ani mā-umaat-nan	'I did not die,
	2	*mā-t-amut		*ati mā-umaat-nan	have not died'
	3 M	*mā-y-amut		etc.	
	F	*mā-t-amut			
Pl	1	*mā-n-amut			
	2	*mā-t-amuut-in			
	3	*mā-y-amuut-in			

(3) *i-verbs: *agis 'to kill'[21]

		Imperfect		Perfect	
Sg	1	*y-agis	'I kill, shall kill'	*y-igis	'I killed, have killed'
	2	*t-agis		*t-igis	
	3 M	*y-agis		*y-igis	
	F	*t-agis		*t-igis	
Pl	1	*n-agis		*n-igis	
	2	*t-agiis-in		*t-igaas-en	
	3	*y-agiis-in		*y-igaas-en	

		Negative Imperfect		Negative Perfect	
Sg	1	*mā-y-agis	'I do, shall not kill'	*ani mā-igas-nan	'I did not kill,
	2	*mā-t-agis		*ati mā-igas-nan	have not killed'
	3 M	*mā-y-agis		etc.	
	F	*mā-t-agis			
Pl	1	*mā-n-agis			
	2	*mā-t-agiis-in			
	3	*mā-y-agiis-in			

Only Rendille has retained all three sets of vowel combinations. The Eastern Sam languages Boni, Jabarti and Somali seem to have reduced them to two: *High - *High for Perfect and *High - *Long Low elsewhere. The latter is derived from the negative Perfect but is now used for all conjugations except the Perfect, i.e. Imperfect as well as all negative paradigms.

Boni has added the aspect markers of Suffix-Verbs to the stem of the Prefix-Verbs (see Heine 1977:34-37). In most dialects of Boni, the negative prefix *mā- has been replaced by h'ū- (and ha- with the Imperative).

3.6.5. Derivation

3.6.5.1. Relationship between Verbs and Nouns

There are a number of Proto-Sam stems which are used both as nouns and verbs, e.g.

*quʃaᶜ	'to cough'	:	*quʃaᶜ	'cough (n)'
*hāb'āàr	'to curse'	:	*hāb'āàr	'curse (n)'

It seems that Proto-Sam had a pattern of deriving verbs from nouns by means of the Causative suffix *-ic (see 3.6.5.2.2), e.g.

*ur F	'smell, odor'	:	*ur-i	'to smell (tr.)'

Other verb-noun relationships observable for Proto-Sam seem to date back to still earlier stages of development in East Cushitic. Thus, the noun *tumaal M 'blacksmith' appears to be derived from the Proto-Sam verb *tum 'to pound', but no regular pattern of derivation of this kind can be established for Proto-Sam.

---

[21]For a discussion of another *i-verb (*imit 'to arrive'), see 4.1.

3.6.5.2. Verbal Suffixes

3.6.5.2.1. Reflexive

The term "Reflexive" is used since this suffix has a function which is similar to that of reflexive forms in various African languages. Furthermore, there are some similarities to reflexive constructions in French and other European languages. Hayward (1975) has proposed "auto-benefactive" and Sim (1977:11) "benefactive", instead.

A sizeable number of Proto-Sam verbs end in *-o, Pl -ɖa. The common denominator of these verbs seems to be that the action expressed by the verb refers to the "logical subject" of the verb which profits from (or is affected by) the action in one or the other way:

*bãħ-s-õ	'to escape'
*baɾ-o	'to learn'
*ɖaq-o	'to accumulate herds'
*gaɾ-o	'to understand'
*gũnt-õ	'to dress oneself'
*d'ĉᶜõ	'to belch'
*q'âb-õ	'to catch, seize, hold'

It must be assumed that Proto-Sam had a suffix *-o expressing reflexive forms of the verb. Boni has retained this suffix as a productive morpheme (see Heine 1977:42). The reflexive function of this ending is evident from examples as the following:

*ɓil	'to comb'	:	*ɓil-o	'to comb oneself'
*gât	'to buy, sell, exchange'	:	*g'ât-õ	'to buy for oneself'
*neeɓ	'breath'	:	*neeɓ-s-o	'to breathe'
*uɾ	'smell (n), odor'	:	*uɾ-s-o	'to smell (tr., i.e. oneself)'

The last two examples suggest that the suffix *-o also functions as a de-nominal derivative suffix. In this case, it is preceded by an element *s.

3.6.5.2.2. Causative

Furthermore, Proto-Sam has a suffix *-ic (*-i in word-final position) which has the function of a Causative morpheme. This suffix is retained as -ic (-i in word-final position) in Rendille (Heine 1976a:40), -i in Somali (Tucker/Bryan 1966:504), and -ii in Jabarti (von Tiling 1921/22:129). Most, if not all, Proto-Sam words ending in *i seem to contain this Causative suffix, e.g.

*ɖaaᶜ-i	'to fall upon'
*ɖaa-i	'to melt (tr.)'
*si-i	'to give'

The derivative function of the suffix *-ic (*-i) is evident from the following examples of Proto-Sam:

*buuħ	'to be full'	:	*bũũħ-i	'to fill'
*kaᶜ	'to stand up'	:	*k'iᶜ-i	'to wake up'
*uɾ	'smell (n), odor'	:	*uɾ-i	'to smell (tr.)'
*bãħ-s-õ	'to escape'	:	*biħ-i	'to take out, pay'

3.6.5.3. Pre-verbal Particles

Proto-Sam must have had a set of particles placed immediately before the verb. The function of these particles is intermediate between nominal prepositions and semantic verbal extensions. Four such particles can be reconstructed, although Proto-Sam must have had a much larger number of them.

3.6.5.3.1. Venitive

All Sam languages have a pre-verbal particle indicating that the action takes place TOWARDS the speaker or deictic focus of the sentence. This Venitive particle has the following shape in the various languages: R *sŏ-*, B *h'ǎ-*, J *sa-* (*ha-*), S *soo*.[22] Proto-Sam is likely to have had **soo* as its Venitive particle of which the Rendille, Jabarti and Somali forms are reflexes.

Two verbs have been reconstructed in their Venitive form:

> **soo noqo* 'to return (intr.)'
> **soo qǎǎt* 'to fetch'   :   **qǎǎt* 'to take, receive'

Somali has, in a similar way as most "Para-Nilotic" and other East African languages, in addition to the Venitive an Andative particle *sii* which indicates the opposite deictic direction, i.e. that the action expressed by the verb takes place AWAY from the speaker or deictic focus of the sentence, e.g.

> *soo so^co* 'to come on'   :   **sii so^co* 'to go on over there'
>   (see Kirk 1905:73/74;
>   Bell 1953:22/23)

There is no other evidence suggesting that Proto-Sam has an Andative particle.

3.6.5.3.2. Ablative

Another particle, which may be labelled "Ablative", has two functions: it indicates either (1) the source ('from, off, away') or (2) the instrument of the action. The assumed Proto-Sam form of this morpheme is **ka* (**ka ~ *ke ~ *ki*). This Ablative has been retained in Rendille (*kǎ-*), Boni (*k'ǐ-, k'ě-, k'ǎ-*) and Jabarti (*ke, ka*). In Somali (*ka*) the morpheme seems to have lost its instrumental function, which is expressed by another particle (*ku*).

The Proto-Sam verb **qǎǎt* 'to take, receive' was frequently used in its Ablative form **ka qǎǎt*, its meaning then being 'to remove'.

3.6.5.3.3. Intransitive

The function of this derivative is to delete the "logical subject" of the sentence without changing its surface case structure, i.e. the "logical object" is not moved to the subject position but remains unaffected by this deletion transformation and is expressed by means of an object in the surface. The Intransitive has been variously called "impersonal passive" (von Tiling 1921/22:146) or "Impersonal" (Tucker/Bryan 1966:524).

The Proto-Sam form of the Intransitive is **la* which has the following reflexes in the modern

---

[22]Note that there are differences concerning the morphological treatment of this particle: whereas in some Somali dialects it seems to be a word of its own, it tends to be used as a verbal prefix elsewhere in the Sam-speaking area.

Sam languages: R *ła-*, B *ł-*, J *ła* (*łe*, *łi*) and S *ła*. In the western Boni area, *ła* has been replaced by *n-*.

One Proto-Sam verb can be reconstructed in its Intransitive form, i.e. *ła-deł* 'to be born', derived from *deł* 'to give birth'.

3.6.5.3.4. Reflexive

In addition to the Reflexive suffix *-o* (see 3.6.5.2.1), Proto-Sam appears to have employed a pre-verbal particle *is* to express a reflexive form of the verb.

This particle is retained in Rendille as *'is-* and in Jabarti as *'is* (von Tiling 1921/22: 119-120). In the other Sam languages *is* has either changed its function or was lost altogether.

3.6.5.4. Frequentative

All Sam languages have a productive mechanism of verb reduplication in order to express the repetition or intensive performance of an act. There are, however, two different morpho-phonemic patterns: in Somali and Jabarti, the whole verb root is reduplicated (Bell 1953: 114; von Tiling 1921/22:129) whereas in Rendille and Boni it is only the initial segment, usually CV-, which is affected, e.g.

R	*usu á-j'áħ-a*	'he hits'	:	*usu á-já-j'áħ-a*	'he hits frequently'
B	*an 'á-'duu'd-a*	'I look at him'	:	*an 'á-'du-'duu'd-a*	'I look at him frequently'
J	*jab*	'to break'	:	*jáb-jab*	'to break into small pieces'
S	*jeeħ*	'to tear'	:	*jeeħ-jeeħ*	'to tear to shreds'

It is possible that both patterns occurred in Proto-Sam. In our sample of reconstructed verbs, the following seem to be the result of reduplication:

ûrûûr-i	'to gather, collect'
daddam-i	'to taste'
gárg'ár	'to help (cf. *gar-o* 'to understand')'
hamhaam-so	'to yawn'

4. THE DEVELOPMENT OF SAM LANGUAGES

In Ch. 3 an attempt has been made at reconstructing grammatical features of Proto-Sam, the hypothetical ancestor language of Rendille, Boni, Jabarti and Somali. In the following, a few details are added concerning the general development of the Sam languages from the time the proto-language was spoken to the present.

4.1. THE FIRST SPLIT OF PROTO-SAM

This split separated Rendille, or Western Sam, from the rest of the Sam languages, referred to here as Eastern Sam, or Dad languages.[23]

---

[23]The name "Dad", first proposed in Heine (1977), is taken from the root *dad* common in Eastern Sam, which means 'man, person'.

Rendille does not seem to have changed very much during its long period of separate development; it has remained the most conservative Sam language. The following phonological changes may be worth mention:

(1) Post-velar stops became fricatives thus giving rise to the sound shifts

$$\left\{ \left[\begin{matrix} *q \\ *' \\ *c \end{matrix} \right]_i \right\}_i \quad > \quad \left\{ \left[\begin{matrix} x \\ \varphi \\ h \end{matrix} \right]_i \right\}_i$$

(2) Proto-Sam $*z$ was palatalized, merging with the semi-vowel y.

The pre-nominal position of the numeral was abandoned in Rendille and the numeral placed after the noun. This development may have been influenced by neighbouring languages (Sampur, Galla, Elmolo) which all place the numeral after the noun it determines.

Another noteworthy development of Rendille can be seen in the generalization of the past demonstrative V $*-ii$ as a gender-sensitive connecting particle linking nouns with adjectives, genitive noun phrases and relative clauses.

The development of the Eastern Sam languages was characterized *inter alia* by the following phonological changes:

(1) The voiceless stops $*t$, $*c$ and $*k$ became voiced morpheme-internally following vowels, thus giving rise to the following shifts:

$$\left\{ \left[\begin{matrix} *t \\ *c \\ *k \end{matrix} \right]_i \right\}_i \quad > \quad \left\{ \left[\begin{matrix} *d \\ *y \\ *g \end{matrix} \right]_i \right\}_i \qquad / \ *V \ \underline{\quad}$$

(2) $*c$ in morpheme-initial position became a fricative ($*sh$).

(3) $*m$ was de-labalized in word-final position and merged with $*n$.

(4) $*z$ merged with $*d$.

A noticeable morphophonological change within Eastern Sam can be seen in the reduction of Prefix-Verb conjugation patterns. Whereas Proto-Sam has three vowel combinations, which have all been retained in Rendille, Eastern Sam has only two combinations (see 3.6.4.2), i.e. the Imperfect vowel pattern *Low - *High has been lost and the pattern *High - *Long Low, which in Proto-Sam is confined to the negative Perfect as well as the Pl 2, 3 of the affirmative Perfect (see 3.6.4.2), is used for the Imperfect. The following reconstructed conjugation patterns of the verb $*imit$ 'to arrive' illustrate this change:

		Proto-Sam	Proto-Eastern Sam
		Imperfect	
Sg	1	$*y\text{-}amit$	$*imaad$
	2	$*t\text{-}amit$	$*t\text{-}imaad$
	3 M	$*y\text{-}amit$	$*y\text{-}imaad$
	F	$*t\text{-}amit$	$*t\text{-}imaad$
Pl	1	$*n\text{-}amit$	$*n\text{-}imaad$
	2	$*t\text{-}amiit\text{-}in$	$*t\text{-}imaad\text{-}in$
	3	$*y\text{-}amiit\text{-}in$	$*y\text{-}imaad\text{-}in$

	Proto-Sam	Proto-Eastern Sam

Perfect

Sg 1	*y-imi(t)	*imi(d)
2	*t-imi(t)	*t-imi(d)
3 M	*y-imi(t)	*y-imi(d)
F	*t-imi(t)	*t-imi(d)
Pl 1	*n-imi(t)	*n-imi(d)
2	*t-imaat-en	*t-imaad-en
3	*y-imaat-en	*y-imaad-en

Negative Perfect

Sg 1	*ani mâ-imaat-nan	*ani mâ-imaad-nan
2	*ati mâ-imaat-nan	*adi mâ-imaad-nan
	etc.	etc.

4.2. THE FIRST SPLIT OF EASTERN SAM

This split separated Boni from all other Eastern Sam languages (Jabarti, Somali and possibly others).

Only after its separation did Boni introduce a number of changes, the most important of which have been outlined in Heine (1977:9-11). They are in particular (see 3.1.1):

(1)   the loss of all pharyngal phonemes (*ᶜ and *ħ (cf. 4.3));

(2)   the loss of the uvular plosive *q;

(3)   The replacement of the voiced plosive *ɖ by the implosive 'd;

(4)   the de-voicing of *d (> t) and *g (> k) in morpheme-initial position and after *r (cf. 4.3);

(5)   the replacement of velar stops (*k and *g) by sh before *i (cf. 4.3);

(6)   the widespread loss of *l, *r and *n in word-final position;

(7)   the labialization of *a (> o/u) preceding *b;

(8)   the shift *ɖ > r in morpheme-internal position following vowels;

(9)   the loss of intervocalic *m in Prefix-Verbs;

(10) the tendency to replace clusters of a nasal followed by another consonant by simple consonants by means of the following rules:

$$\text{(i)}\quad [+ \text{nas}]\quad \begin{bmatrix} - \text{voc} \\ + \text{cons} \\ + \text{voic} \end{bmatrix}\quad \rightarrow \quad [+ \text{nas}]$$

$$\text{(ii)}\quad [+ \text{nas}]\quad \rightarrow \quad \phi\ /\ \underline{\quad\quad}\ \begin{bmatrix} - \text{voc} \\ + \text{cons} \\ - \text{voic} \end{bmatrix}$$

(11) the reduction of nominal number distinctions;

(12) the loss of the distinction Inclusive/Exclusive in Pl 1 personal pronouns.

Changes that took place in the Jabarti-Somali branch of Eastern Sam seem to include the following:

(1) The Proto-Sam demonstratives II *-a and V *-ii (see 3.3.3.3) became Deictic Determiners.

(2) The conjugation patterns of Prefix-Verbs disappeared largely, leaving only a few fossilized paradigms.

4.3. THE SECOND SPLIT OF EASTERN SAM

This split lead to a separation of early "southern Somali", represented linguistically by Jabarti, from "Somali proper".

Changes that affected Jabarti have been summarized in some detail by von Tiling (1921/22). The most striking developments are:

(1) the loss of pharyngal consonants;

(2) the replacement of *ɖ by a liquid (ɾ) following vowels;

(3) the replacement of *k by ʃh before front vowels.

These changes have occurred in a similar, though not identical, form in Boni (see 4.2) and it would seem that they are due to an areal relationship which developed after the first split of Eastern Sam in the area between the Tana and Shebelle rivers.

Other developments in Jabarti are:

(4) the velarization of word-final nasals (*m, *n > ŋ);

(5) the reduction of demonstrative categories to two (see 3.3.3.3; Table 2);

(6) the merger of the Durative marker *-ay with the Imperfect suffix *-a (von Tiling 1921/22: 130-33);

(7) phonological contractions in the formation of noun plurals.

The development of Somali was characterized in particular by the following changes:

(1) the widespread loss of pharyngal consonants if preceded and followed by *a;

(2) the introduction of thematic particles preceding the verb in finite sentences. These particles, which are commonly referred to as Indicators, are waa, baa (yaa, ayaa), ma and ha (see Tucker/Bryan 1966:541-42);

(3) the addition of an Andative derivative ʃii ("movement away") to complement the Proto-Sam Venitive *ʃoo (see 3.6.5.3.1).

5. NOTES ON HISTORY

Research on the history of Sam-speaking people has so far concentrated on one of these groups, the Somali. There is a remarkable amount of disagreement as to the earlier homeland of the Somali people. Murdock (1959:319) claims that until the second half of the first millenium they, together with the Afar and Galla, were confined to southeastern Ethiopia, east of the great Rift Valley. Ehret (1974:34) assumes that the ancestors of modern Somali and Rendille left the southern edges of the Ethiopian Highlands and entered the Kenya-Somalia borderlands roughly a thousand years ago. According to I.M. Lewis (1960:216) again, the Somali lived at that time thousands of kilometres away from that area in the north-eastern part of the Horn. Harold C. Fleming, on the other hand, considers the low-land area between Lake Turkana (Rudolf) on the west and the Benadir coast on the east, from the Tana river in the south to the Ogaden in the north as the earlier homelands (Fleming 1964:84).

Disagreement also exists concerning the socio-economic structure of the early Somali society. Murdock maintains that they were practicing agriculture supplemented by animal husbandry and by commerce with the coastal towns. This tallies with Harold Fleming's observation that they adopted their camel economy only later at roughly the same time with acquiring Islam (Fleming 1964:86). Other accounts again suggest that Somali economy has been based on nomadic pastoralism from the earliest times (see below).

But the most divergent views have been expressed concerning the direction of early Somali migrations. I.M. Lewis and Enrico Cerulli claim that the conquest of the Horn started in the north and proceded southwards. Fleming, who does not dispute that such migrations took place, suggests that they involved the Daarood clan-family only and that they were preceded by earlier south-north movements in which the whole Somali people took part (Fleming 1964: 84). A similar view has been expressed by Sasse (1975:20).

In the following, an attempt is made at drawing some conclusions from our linguistic analysis concerning the history and migration patterns of the Sam-speaking people as a whole. Our research suggests that any attempt at writing on the early history of the Somali nation must remain fragmentary unless due consideration is given to its closest relatives, in particular the Boni and Rendille.

For the larger part of this history, there exist no written records whatsoever and the scope of oral traditions usually does not extend beyond the last few centuries. Thus, next to archeology, linguistics is the most important source of information on the early Sam history.

There are, however, some fundamental shortcomings in the following discussion. The first relates to the fact that we have to confine ourselves to only one aspect of history which is reflected in DIVERGENT linguistic development. An attempt at describing CONVERGENT developments, as reflected, e.g. in lexical borrowing, will not be made in this paper.

The second shortcoming is inherent in all linguistic comments on essentially extra-linguistic processes. The tools available to the linguist allow him access to a restricted range of facts only, and the resulting interpretation of history is therefore likely to differ from that of, say, an "oral historian", who, due to the nature of his data, focusses on quite different aspects of historical reality. Although we claim that both approaches are equally valid we are aware of the fact that the interpretation of the linguist may lead to a simplified, and in extreme cases even a distorted, picture of certain historical events.

5.1. EAST CUSHITIC EXPANSIONS

Proto-Sam, the hypothetical ancestor language of Rendille, Boni and the Somali group, is a member of a larger language group for which we have proposed the name Omo-Tana (Heine 1976b). All Omo-Tana languages, with the exception of the Sam languages, are spoken between Lake Abaya and Lake Turkana. This suggests fairly strongly that the homeland of the Omo-Tana-speaking people should have been in roughly this area, i.e. east of the Omo River in the lacustrine belt stretching from Lake Zwai in the north to Lake Turkana in the southwest. It is this general area where the "origin" of other East Cushitic populations,[24] and probably of East Cushitic as a whole, has to be located, as the present distribution and the network of historical relationship between the East Cushitic languages suggest.

The subsequent development of these populations is characterized *inter alia* by an expansion towards the lowlands north, east and south of the Ethiopian Highlands. The following groups participated in this spread:

(1)   The SAHO and AFAR who seem to have migrated in north-eastern direction. It is very likely that they still formed one people when they reached the plains (H.S. Lewis 1966: 41).

(2)   The OMO-TANA-speaking people, with the exception of the Bayso (Baiso) and possibly other groups. They spread south in two apparently independent movements: one segment, which is represented today by Galaboid-speaking people, settled between Lake Stefanie and Lake Turkana. Two of these people, the Arbore and Dasenech (Galeb, Reshiat, Shangila), are found today in this general area. A third people, the Elmolo, followed the eastern shore of Lake Turkana up to its southern end and became fishermen. The second movement of Omo-Tana-speaking populations involves the early Sam community (see 5.2).

(3)   The YAAKU (Mogogodo). No specific clues concerning their migrations are available so far. We must assume that they proceeded straight south across the arid plains of northern Kenya and settled in the hilly country north of Mt. Kenya, adopting a hunter-gatherer existence.[25]

(4)   The GALLA (Oromo). They expanded in all directions except west, following mostly the routes that other East Cushitic communities (Saho-Afar in the north, and Sam in the south) appear to have chosen before them.

More recent research (Haberland 1963; H.S. Lewis 1966; Turton 1975) suggests that of all these movements towards the lowlands it was the Galla expansion that took place last, perhaps over a millenium later than the other expansions.[26] A relative chronology of these various lowland migrations does not yet seem possible. The fact that the Sam-speaking Rendille figure prominently in the oral traditions of the Yaaku (Heine 1975:30) may indicate that these two groups moved south at about the same time, but this is only one of several possibilities. Whether the Afar-Saho migrated out of the East Cushitic homelands prior to the Omo-Tana communities, as H.S. Lewis (1966:41-2) suggests, remains to be investigated. Lewis bases his hypothesis on the observation that the linguistic differentiation between Afar and Saho is greater than between the various Somali dialects, thus suggesting a higher age of separation for the former. But Lewis does not take into consideration that the Somali were only one part of a larger community which includes among others Rendille and Boni. The time depth of separation between these groups is certainly greater than that between Afar and Saho.[27]

---

[24]The Galla, for example, are said to have originated in north-west Borana between Lake Shamo and Lake Stefanie (H.S. Lewis 1966.41).

[25]Today, they inhabit the Mukogodo Forest of Laikipia-District, where they are being absorbed both linguistically and culturally by their Maasai-speaking neighbours (see Heine 1975).

[26]It would seem that the Galla were largely confined to their homeland in South Ethiopia until about 1530 (see H.S. Lewis 1966:27).

[27]Note, however, that this discussion does not prove much, if anything at all. There need not be a correlation between the age of migration and the degree of linguistic differentiation in this special case, since it is not possible to infer WHERE the process of language separation started.

5.2. PROTO-SAM

Of all East Cushitic migrations away from the South Ethiopian Highlands that of the Sam-speaking people turned out to be the most successful in terms of territorial expansion. One may say in fact that sub-Suharan Africa has experienced only few migrations within a relatively short time span involving such a wide territory.[28]

It is in the plains to the south of the Ethiopian Highlands east of Lake Turkana where the homeland of the Sam-speaking people has to be located and it is from there that the early migrations towards the south started.

This view differs slightly from that of Fleming (1964:87) who claims a more north-easterly origin for his "Macro-Somali" community.[29] Fleming's reconstruction is based on his "discovery" of Bayso, a language spoken of Gidicho Island in Lake Abaya. Since Bayso is not related to Somali as closely as was suggested by Fleming, i.e. it is certainly NOT a member of the Sam group, it can largely remain out of consideration in a discussion on the Proto-Sam homelands. Judging from the present distribution of the Sam languages and their genetic relationship patterns, the following conclusion seems obvious: the Sam homeland must be sought around or near the area where the first split of Proto-Sam occurred. This split, which separated Rendille from the rest of the Sam languages, is likely to have taken place somewhere along the south-eastern border of the Rendille-speaking country. The Proto-Sam homelands must therefore be located to the south of the Ethiopian Highlands in the general area of north-central Kenya, perhaps in the plains surrounding the Marsabit Plateau.

The hypothetical Proto-Sam-speaking community was typically one of camel breeders. The camel was probably acquired in the plains of North Kenya after the descent from the Ethiopian Highlands, and it enabled the Sam-speaking people to conquer all the arid areas between Lake Turkana and the Zeila coast of North Somalia.[30]

The existence of a camel economy is suggested by the presence of a specialized Proto-Sam vocabulary involving camels. So far, the following items have been reconstructed: *gaal 'camel', *âûr 'male camel', *hal 'female camel', *q'áálîm 'young male camel', *qâál'îm 'young female camel', *kor 'camel-bell', and *kurs- 'hump of camel'.

The assumption that Proto-Sam was overwhelmingly, or exclusively, a pastoral society is supported by the presence of reconstructed items like *daqo 'to accumulate herds', *foofi 'to send (herds) out to graze', *tum 'to castrate by crushing', or *maal 'to milk'. Compared to camels, cattle seem to have been of secondary, if of any, importance--the Proto-Sam lexicon being much less specific about them.

---

[28]Although less spectacular both in the number of people involved and in the territory covered, the Sam migrations show several parallels to the Bantu expansion in southern Africa (see below).

[29]It would seem that this divergence is to some extent due to differences in languages classification: Fleming's "Macro-Somali" is more comprehensive than our Sam group. It includes Bayso which is an Omo-Tana but not a Sam language, and it excludes the Galaboid group which, according to the evidence presented by Sasse (1975), belongs to Omo-Tana. This difference has various implications for the territorial history of "Macro-Somali" (see below).

[30]Whereas the reconstruction of a camel economy for the Proto-Sam community rests on very strong linguistic evidence, there are no linguistic clues as to who introduced the camel in Eastern Africa, and FROM WHOM did the early Sam people acquire them.

The only reconstructed items in our list are *sa^c 'cow' and *loi^ɔ 'cattle'. The presence of sheep and goats is attested by Proto-Sam words like *aḍi 'sheep and goats', *maqal 'young sheep and goats', *ri 'goat', *waħ'ár 'kid', *laħ 'ewe', and *saber 'virgin ewe'.

Agriculture was known but probably not practiced. There is a word *qut meaning both 'to dig' and 'to cultivate', but the word *bèèr 'garden' is confined to Eastern Sam.

It is likely that the Proto-Sam-speaking people practiced circumcision and buried their dead, as is suggested by words like *gut 'to circumcise', *ħàw'áàl 'to bury', and *ħawaal 'grave', though no more specific information is available. Perhaps more significant is the observation that the Proto-Sam community was familiar with iron-work, words like *bir 'iron' and *tumaal 'blacksmith' having been retained all over the Sam-speaking area.[31]

Any attempt at dating early Sam history must remain tentative at the present stage of research. Glottochronological calculations suggest that the common ancestor language of the modern Sam languages is at least between 1700 and 2300 years old, i.e. that the hypothetical Proto-Sam community dates back to roughly the beginning of the Christian era.[32]

This would mean that of all populations found today in northern Kenya, Sam-speaking people were the first to settle there, probably with the exception of the Yaaku (see 5.1). Provided that this date is confirmed by further research, this would also mean that a knowledge of iron-working is likely to have existed in northern Kenya before the Christian era.

And the same applies, of course, to camel economy. The Sam-speaking area constitutes one of the best camel regions of the world, and the Eastern Sam territory, i.e. Somalia, has probably the densest camel population in Africa (cf. Epstein 1971, II:551). The one-humped camel (dromedary) was domesticated in Central and Southern Arabia as early as 1800 B.C., if not earlier (Zeuner s.a.:297), and it was introduced from there in eastern and north-eastern Africa. According to Reinhard Walz (1951:41; 1954), it reached the Horn of Africa during the middle of the first millenium B.C., or even 300 to 400 years earlier. Thus, Sam-speaking people must have taken up camel breeding before the animal was introduced in Egypt (Epstein

---

[31] The regularity of sound correspondences suggests that these words can be traced back to the Proto-Sam community. Archeological evidence, on the other hand, suggests that iron is of extremely recent introduction to the north Kenya plains (David Phillipson; personal communication of 19-10-1976).

[32] The common percentages of basic vocabulary between the three main Sam languages are:

	100-word list	200-word list
Rendille-Somali	51%	46%
Rendille-Boni	50%	47%
Somali-Boni	59%	56%

Using the glottochronological formula $t = \dfrac{\log C}{2 \log r}$ the following figures of time depth result:

	100-word list	200-word list
Rendille-Somali	2,228 years	1,790 years
Rendille-Boni	2,295 years	1,740 years
Somali-Boni	1,748 years	1,337 years

Thus, we may assume that the separation between Western and Eastern Sam occurred approximately between 300 B.C. and 200 A.D. Since this date marks the end of the Proto-Sam period, the hypothetical ancestor language must be assumed to be even older than that. The first split within Eastern Sam, i.e. between Boni and Jabarti-Somali, appears to have taken place between 200 A.D. and 600 A.D.

1971, II:565). We are led to assume that the Proto-Sam-speaking people met the camel after having left the Ethiopian Highlands when they began to establish themselves in the plains of northern Kenya. Subsequently, the ecomomy, culture and social life of the Sam people became focussed on the camel.

5.3. EARLY SAM MIGRATIONS

Roughly at the beginning of the Christian era, probably during the first three centuries A.D., the Proto-Sam-speaking people began to spread in a south-eastern direction.[33] These movements led past the Lorian Swamps to the Tana River and along its eastern banks to the Indian Ocean, thus making the whole of north-eastern Kenya, from Lake Turkana to the Lamu Archipelago a Sam-speaking territory.

Whereas the linguistic analysis (see 4.1) suggests a clear-cut split between the Western and the Eastern Sam people, the actual development was probably more complex: it was a gradual expansion involving the more active segments of the population rather than a sudden separation. By approximately 500 A.D., we may assume, there existed a continuum of more or less independent Sam groups speaking mutually intelligible dialects, stretching from Lake Turkana to the sea shores. The extreme ends of this dialect continuum became more and more different up to the point that linguistic communication was rendered difficult. The western dialects developed into a language of its own which is nowadays known as Rendille. These dialects were probably linked with the eastern dialects by a chain of intelligibility until they were separated by the intrusion of the Galla in the 16th century (see 5.6).

The Western Sam (Rendille) roughly maintained their territory up to the present. At times in history, they experienced population movements ranging from the Ethiopian Highlands in the north to the mountainous areas of Sampur country in the south. Around 1820 they are said to have been concentrated on the Lbarta Plains and in the Suguta Valley, but twenty years later they are reported to have migrated back into their present territory driving the Laikipiak Maasai southwards (Spencer 1973:150, 152).

The Eastern Sam continued with their migrations in the same way as earlier Sam people: once a new territory was occupied, part of the population would settle down whereas another part moved on looking for new grazing areas. The Sam-speaking area thus was continually extended. This pattern of territorial expansion is clearly reflected in the pattern of genetic relationship. It is the same pattern that has been observed in the spread of the Bantu people during the last two millenia[34] (cf. Heine et al. 1975).

---

[33]Most probably, this was not the only direction of spread. Conceiveably, the south and east were other directions of Sam expansion, but if it was so, then such movements were superseded by later immigrations of both other East Cushites and Nilotes.

[34]This development can be represented in a simplified form thus:

$$A - B_1 \quad B_2 - C_1 \quad C_2 - D_1 \quad D_2$$

'A' would be the "original" group. B_1 is that part of A that stayed behind whereas B_2 left the homeland to look for a new settlement area. C_1 settled in this new area whereas C_2 split off and established new homes farther away. This new C_2 territory became the

Upon reaching the coastal area, the expansion of Eastern Sam people proceeded in a northern direction into what is today the Republic of Somalia. The linguistic history records two important break-offs from the main stream of expansion. The first involves those groups that, due to unknown circumstances, were forced to give up animal husbandry and decided on a hunter-gatherer existence in the forest belt of the coastal hinterland north of the Tana River. They are the only Eastern Sam people on Kenyan territory that survived the invasion of the Galla. Their modern descendants are the various Boni-speaking groups.

The second major section that stayed behind, and became largely sedentary, is represented linguistically by "Jabarti". This section appears to have settled first along the lower course of the Juba River where it replaced its traditional nomadic pastoralism by a mixed economy which focussed more and more on agriculture. The settlement area of the "Jabarti"-speaking cluster was gradually extended to cover most of the fertile lands between and including the Juba and Shebelle Rivers. The evidence available suggests that the pre-Hawiyye (pre-Hawiya) mentioned by Colucci (1924:91) and Turton (1975) constituted a major branch of this section.

One Eastern Sam section, however, continued to expand in a northern direction by crossing the Shebelle River and penetrating into the Horn of East Africa. This section, which came to be known as Samaale or "Somali proper", maintained its traditional camel economy, and its territorial and political development accounts for most of what is nowadays known as the history of the Somali and the history of the East African Horn.

5.4. THE "ABORIGINAL POPULATION" OF THE HORN

Most, though not all, scholars commenting on Somali history agree that the East African Horn, and in particular the southern part of it, was inhabited by a "Negro" population, before it was conquered by East Cushitic nomads. This "aboriginal population", as I.M. Lewis (1955: 45) calls it, is said to have contained at least two culturally divergent groups: the major segment consisted of "cultivators living as sedentaries along the Juba and Shebelle Rivers and in fertile pockets between them" (Lewis 1960:216).

The second group was made up of nomadic hunters and fishermen, often possessing dogs. According to I.M. Lewis, the Ribi and Boni of Jubaland and Southern Somalia, though modified by Cushitic influence, are modern descendents of these hunters (Lewis 1960:216). It would seem that this statement is not quite corroborated by linguistic findings (see 5.3).

These "Negroid populations" are referred to collectively by medieval Arab writers as *Zengi* (blacks). They probably did not extend north of the Shebelle River at that time.

---

homeland of D_1 whereas D_2, another offshoot of C_2, pushed on and conquered new lands.

The development of Sam languages is very much in accordance with this model: Rendille (B_1) and Eastern Sam (B_2) are descendents of Proto-Sam (A). Eastern Sam split into Boni (C_1) and "Jabarti-Somali" (C_2) with the latter group again splitting into those that stayed behind (i.e. "Jabarti"; D_1) and those that proceded further ("Somali proper"; D_2). In the case of Bantu history, the model is the same, the only difference being that the number of descendent groups was usually higher than two, i.e.

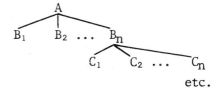

etc.

Our knowledge about the early inhabitants of the Horn is scanty, to say the least. Linguistic evidence suggests that Bantu people were NOT among them. Contrary to the view expressed by I.M. Lewis (1960:216), according to which the pre-Cushitic cultivators living along the Juba and Shebelle Rivers were partly Bantu, there is every reason to assume that Bantu-speaking communities like Pokomo, northern Swahili (Bajuni, Miini, et al.), or Shebeli, Shidle and Gosha met already Sam-speaking people north of River Tana when they arrived there.[35] George Peter Murdock estimates that the Bantu reached the Somalia coast in the second half of the first millenium.[36] By this time, the early Somali are likely to have extended at least as far north as River Shebelle (see below).

If there were no Bantu people who preceded the Eastern Cushities in the Horn, the question is who the other people referred to by I.M. Lewis may have been. Fleming (1964:92) notes that the assumption of a Negro priority in the Horn is not supported archeologically. Oral traditions do not seem to shed any light on this problem, mainly because of the time depth involved. Linguistics does not offer any noticeable clues either. The presence of Dahalo near the mouth of River Tana might imply that Southern Cushites, possibly intermingled with Khoisan-speaking groups, extended as far north as Somalia. But it is equally possible that large parts of the Horn were uninhabited by the time the East Cushitic pastoralists occupied it.[37]

For some time, it has been suggested that the first wave of East Cushites to take possession of the Horn consisted of Galla groups who superseded earlier populations there. G.W.B. Huntingford notes:

> "It is clear that the first African homeland of the Galla was what is now British Somaliland and northern Somalia, to which their own traditions bring them; these traditions are confirmed by the attribution to the Galla by the Somali of most of the cairns and other ruins in Somaliland, and there can in fact be little doubt that the Galla occupation here preceded that of the Soamli." (Huntingford 1955:19)

I.M. Lewis, who adopted this view, points out that residual pockets of Galla are still found amongst the northern Somali, especially in the western and Ogaden region (Lewis 1960:219).

This hypothesis has been refuted more recently by scholars working on Somali history (H.S. Lewis 1966; Turton 1975). Linguistically, there is nothing to suggest that the Eastern Sam expansion was preceded by an earlier Galla occupation of the Horn (see 5.1).

5.5. THE OCCUPATION OF THE HORN

Within a relatively short period the Samaale or "Somali proper" overflooded and occupied

---

[35] The degree of linguistic differentiation is the main argument here. Harold Fleming summarizes it thus: "The differences within Somali generally (Rendille, Boni, and Somali proper) distinctly exceed those obtaining among the Coastal Bantu and are not greatly exceeded by East African Bantu differentiation generally" (Fleming 1964:92). See also Turton (1975).

[36] "At some time early in the second half of the first millenium, ... the agricultural Bantu, who had recently arrived in East Africa, spread north eastward along the coast of Somali and occupied the fertile valleys of the Juba and Shebelle Rivers, driving the indigenous hunters into the arid sections of the interior" (Murdock 1959:319).

[37] Note, however, that there is archeological evidence for fairly recent Late Stone Age peoples in the Horn (David Phillipson; personal communication of 19-10-1976).

the whole of the Horn. If there existed any earlier populations on the peninsula they were either driven away, or absorbed both linguistically and culturally. By around 1000 A.D., if not earlier, the first phase of Eastern Sam migrations was completed. The Somali had spread all along what Arab writers referred to as the "Zayla coast" (Lewis 1960:217-218).

Probably from 700 A.D. onwards, Arabs and Persians had begun to establish strongholds along the shores of the Horn. From their intercourse with the Somali pastoralists arriving from the south, a new Islamic culture and society emerged, in which Arab traders and proselytisers formed an aristocracy. This culture appears to have been largely urban in outlook. The port towns of Zeila and Berbera were founded before the turn of the first post-Christian millenium, and a series of other settlements appeared all along the east coast, among them Mogadishu, Merca and Brava. One important basis of this culture was the trade between the African hinterland and Arabia. Especially Zeila developed into a flourishing trading center. I.M. Lewis records:

> "This town was politically the most important of the Arab settlements in the north and owed its economic prosperity to its geographical position as one of the chief ports of early Abyssinia in the trade with Arabia and the Orient. Through Zeila local Somali produce, consisting chiefly of hides and skins, precious gums, ghee, and ostrich feathers, and slaves and ivory from the Abyssinian hinterland, was exported; and cloth, dates, iron, weapons, and chinaware and pottery imported. Politically Zeila was originally the centre of the Muslim emirate of Adal, part of the state of Ifāt, which lay in the plateau region of eastern Shoa. From the period at which the port enters Islamic history it had apparently a mixed Arab, Somali and 'Afar population .... In the course of time, no one knows exactly when, these three elements fused to form a distinctive Zeila culture and a Zeila dialect which was a blend of Arabic, Somali and 'Afar." (Lewis 1960:217-218).

By the 12th century A.D. the whole of the northern coast had been Islamized, as is claimed by the Arab historian Yaqut, and the ground had been prepared for Muslim expansion further inland (Huntingford 1955:19).

5.6.   SOUTHERN MIGRATION

After having conquered most, if not all, parts of the Horn, we notice that from the beginning of the second millenium the direction of migrations was reversed: Muslim Somali groups leave the northern and eastern coasts and migrate south. The motives of this movement are still largely unclear. I.M. Lewis suggests that increased immigration from Arabia was a contributing factor (I.M. Lewis 1960:220), but proselytism probably also played a role. As early as the tenth or eleventh century, Sheikh Ismaa'iil Jabartii had arrived from Arabia and became the founder of the Daarood clan-family in north-eastern Somalia. He was followed some 200 years later by Sheikh Isaaq who founded another major clan-family of Somali, the Isaaq who settled to the west of the Daarood.

The advance towards the south is described by I.M. Lewis in some detail (I.M. Lewis 1960:220 ff.). The Muslim Somali seem to have followed two main routes, either along the Indian Ocean coast following the Shebelle River and its tributaries downwards, or in the western interior where they were brought in conflict with the Christian empire of Ethiopia.

In the south, groups of Hawiyye pushed towards and crossed the Shebelle River, overpowering non-Islamic earlier Sam residents like the Ajuraan in the 17th century. I.M. Lewis concludes from local traditions that the area between Shebelle and Juba to the south of Bur Hacaba was in the possession of the Galla, but it seems likely that the predominant population of that region were Jabarti-speaking Sam.

In the meantime, the Galla had begun to expand from their South Ethiopian homeland in all directions except west. It was especially the migrations of the Orma, probably starting in Dirre, which affected the more recent history of various Sam groups. The Orma claim to have moved via Moyale to the Lorian Swamps, one branch of them pushing south to the Tana River and down to the Indian Ocean (Turton 1975:532 ff.).

Although the evidence on the history of the Southern Galla is to some extent controversial, some general statements concerning the development of subsequent Galla-Sam relations seem possible:

(1) The southern migrations of the Galla concluded the territorial separation between the Western Sam (Rendille) and the Eastern Sam.

(2) The Orma largely followed routes taken by the earliest Eastern Sam people, absorbing parts of them and driving others north in the direction of the Juba River.

(3) Later on, after the Sam country north of the Tana River had largely become Galla-speaking, the Galla collided with the Islamized northern Somali who were flooding south. At first, the Daarood-Somali were seeking alliance with the Galla, but later they fought them and drove them southwards. After having crossed the Juba River, groups of Daarood reached the western banks of the Tana River in 1909, subjugating local Orma communities.

The major Somali migrations were brought to a standstill by the British colonial government, although, as I.M. Lewis (1960:222-225) observes, Somali infiltration southwards still continues today.

6. COMPARATIVE VOCABULARY

The following is a list of reconstructed Proto-Sam roots. Concerning the transcription and abbreviations used, see 3. For transcription, see Table 1, p. 11.

*aab- M 'father'
  R ába
  S aabbe M
  J áâw M

*aqal M 'house'
  S aqal M, Pl aqalo F
  J agál M

*aayo 'mother'
  R 'áyo
  B aay'ô

*abees- F 'viper spec.'
  R eb'ēsa, Pl ebesay'ô F/M
  S abeeso F, Pl abeesoyin M 'viper, serpent, monster'

*aboor M 'termites'
  S aboor 'white ants'
  B ab'oor M

*addin M 'leg'
  S addin M
  B 'iddi , Pl 'iddiin^e M/Pl

*adañ, Pl *adañ-o F/M 'back (n)'
  R aḍ'áñ, Pl adañ'ô F/M
  S adañ F, Pl adño 'backbone'

*ad̪i̧ M 'sheep and goats'   R   'ad̪i̧ M
                                        S   ad̪i̧ M
                                        J   ir̂i̧
                                        B   'ir̂e M

*aɓ M 'mouth'   R   aɓ M
                                        S   aɓ M
                                        B   âɓ M

aɓ M 'language', cf. 'mouth'   R   aɓ M
                                        S   aɓ M
                                        B   âɓ M

*'âɓar̂ 'four'   R   'âɓar̂; aɓ'âr̂
                                        S   aɓar̂ F
                                        J   âɓar̂
                                        B   âɓar̂

*agis 'to kill', see 3.6.4.2   R   agis
                                        B   iis/iaas

*agor̂, Pl *agor̂-o M/F 'calf-sized   R   og'ôr̂, Pl ogor̂'ô 'gazelle (gen.)'
    animal'   S   agor̂ M, Pl agor̂o 'bull calf to two years old'

*-ah̃a 'your (Sg possess.)'   R   -ah̃a
                                        S   -aa
                                        J   -aa
                                        B   -aha; -a'

*ah̃am 'to eat', see 3.6.4.2   R   ah̃am
                                        B   ahaŋ

*amaah 'to borrow water'   R   am'âh
                                        S   amaaho 'to borrow'

*amut 'to die', see 3.6.4.2   R   amut
                                        B   uud/uaad

*'ângèg 'dry'   R   'ângag
                                        S   engeg-an
                                        B   'âneg M 'dryness'

*ani, *an 'I'   R   ani; an
                                        S   an'i-ga M; aan
                                        J   âni
                                        B   ani; an

*ar̂g/'âr̂gâ 'to see'   R   'âgar̂/'âr̂ga
                                        S   ar̂ag
                                        B   'âr̂k/'âr̂ka

*ar̂it, Pl ar̂it-o F/M 'gate of   R   ar̂'it, Pl ar̂it'ô
    animal pan'   S   ir̂id-i, Pl ir̂ido M

*ati, *at 'you (Sg)'   R atí; at
                                       S adî-ga M; aad
                                       J 'ãdí
                                       B ati, adi; at, ad

*atin 'you (Pl)'   R atín
                                       S idîn-ka M; aydín

*ãũr M 'male camel'   R ôr, Pl our'ãr, ouru'ãr M/M 'bull camel, bull'
                                       S awr M, Pl awr F
                                       B ôor M 'male elephant'

*-ay 'my'   R -aya
                                       S -ay
                                       J -ee
                                       B -e

*baal, Pl *baal-al 'leaf, feather'   S baal M, Pl baalal 'feather'
                                       B b'âal M 'feather'; bâsh, Pl bale F/Pl 'leaf'

*babaᶜ F 'palm (of hand)'   S babaᶜo F
                                       B bᵉb'a' F; buba' F (Ed)

*bahal 'poisonous snake (spec.)'   S bahal M, Pl bahalo F 'wild animal'
                                       B b'ãhal F

*bãñs-ð 'to escape'   R bañso/bañs'ãda
                                       S bañso

*bakaal 'bright star'   S bakal 'Venus' (Fleming 1964:70)
                                       B bak'ãal M

*ballaad- 'wide'   R ball'ãdí
                                       S ballaad-an; balad-an

*barar 'to swell'   S barar
                                       B bar'êr/bar'êêra'; barar- (Ed)

*barbar M 'shoulder'   R b'ãrbar, Pl barb'ãrre M/F
                                       S barbar M, Pl barbaro F 'side'

*bari 'east'   R ber'í
                                       S bari

*barkey 'headrest'   S barki M, Pl barkiyo F 'wooden pillow'
                                       B barkᵉ F
                                       J barshi

*bar-o 'to learn'   S baro
                                       B baro/bar'ê'da

*bat-an 'many'   S badan
                                       B b'adᵉ
                                       J bazãŋ

*bĕen F 'lie (n)'   R b'ĕēn, Pl been'ŏ F/M
                                           S been F
                                           B b'ĕe F; b'ĕen F (E)

*bĕeʁ M 'liver'   S beeʁ M
                                           B b'ĕeʁ M (E)

*bèèʁ, Pl *bèèʁ-o F/M 'garden'   S beeʁ, Pl beeʁo
                                           B beeʁ, Pl beeʁᵉ F/Pl

*bez F 'lake'   R bey, Pl bey'ăy F/M
                                           S bad F

*bice(o)' M 'water'   R bic'ĕ, Pl bicey'ŏ M/M
                                           S biiyo M
                                           J biiyŏŏ M
                                           B biy'o M

*biñ-ɨ 'to take out, pay'   R biñi 'to give out'
                                           S biñi
                                           B b'ɨhi/bih'ɨa

*bil(-ta) F 'month'   S bil (-sha)
                                           B bil, bɨsh (← *bil-t) F

*bilig 'flash (lightning)'   S bilig F
                                           B bilikso 'lightning'

*bin'ă M 'dangerous wild animal'   R bin'ă M
                                           B bin'ănsᵉ M

*biʁ F 'iron'   R biʁ F
                                           S biʁ-ta
                                           B biʁ F 'iron point of arrow'

*bitañ 'left (side)'   S bidiñ F
                                           B bidah

*bood 'dust'   S bood M
                                           B booʁ F

*boqol 'hundred'   S boqol M
                                           J bogŏl
                                           cf. B b'ŏk'ol

*bud(-ka) M 'club'   S bud M
                                           B b'ŭkkᵉ (← *b'ŭ'd-kᵉ) M

*bun M 'coffee bean' (loanword)   R bun M
                                           S bun M 'coffee'
                                           B bûŋ M

*buuñ 'to be full'   R buñ
                                           S buuñ-so; buñ
                                           B b'ŭŭh-ɨ 'to fill' (see *bŭŭñ-ɨ)

*búúñ-ì/bùùñ-'ícǎ 'to fill'   R búñi
                                        S buuñi
                                        B b'úúñi/bùùh'ía

*buur 'big (of things)'   R buur, Pl ab'uur
                                        S buur-an 'stout'

*cab'eel M 'leopard'   S shabeel M
                                        J shiβéél
                                        B shub'éel M
                                        cf. R kab'íl, Pl kabil'ô M/M

*can 'five'   R cán F
                                        S shan F
                                        J shaŋ
                                        B shâŋ

*ceek 'to tell'   R cek
                                        S sheeg; sheg
                                        J sheeg
                                        B shée

*celei 'yesterday'   R cel'é
                                        S shalei; sheley
                                        B shâlé; sh'élé (E)

*cit 'to light'   S shid-i 'to light, kindle'
                                        B shîd/sh'ída

*cilim F 'tick (parasite)'   R cil'ím, Pl cilim'ám F/M
                                        S shilin F, Pl shilimo 'small tick'
                                        B shílmí F

*cimbir, Pl cimbir-o F/M 'bird'   R cimbír, Pl cimbir'ô F/M
                                        S shimbir F, Pl shimbiro
                                        B sh'ímir F

*cinni, Pl cinni-yo F/M 'bee'   R cínni, Pl cinniy'ô F/M
                                        S shinni F, Pl shinniyo M

*cub 'to pour'   S shub
                                        B k'í-shub/ki-sh'úa (see 3.6.5.3.2)

*dáàr 'to touch'   R dâr; dâr
                                        B t'áar/t'áára

*dab 'to plait'   R dab-i
                                        B tob/t'óba; tub (Ed)

*dab, Pl dab-ab M/M 'fire'   R dab, Pl dab'áb M/M
                                        S dab M, Pl dabab
                                        B tób M

*dab 'to set a trap'   S dab-i 'to trap, catch unaware, snare'
                                        B tuub; tub (Ed)

*dab-in 'trap (n)'   S   dabin M
                                            B   t'oun F

*dad M 'person'   S   dâd-ki
                                            J   dâd-ki
                                            cf. B dad, Pl d'ãgg^e M/F

*daib M 'tail'   R   dub, Pl dub'âb M/F
                                            S   dabo F, Pl daboyin M
                                            B   tib, Pl tibt^e M/M

*dammaal 'to swim'   S   dabaalo
                                            B   duumaal (Ed)

*-dar 'to add'   S   ku dar-i
                                            B   ke-tar (Ed)

*dawaᶜo F 'jackal'   R   dow'õño, Pl dow'õñoyõ F/M
                                            S   dawaᶜo F, Pl dawaᶜayal F;
                                                daᶜawo F, Pl daᶜawoyin M

*daᵓ 'to rain'   R   d'ãto
                                            B   taᵓ
                                            J   daᵓ

*d'ê^ᶜ-ô/*dê^ᶜ-ô-dã 'to belch'   R   d'êño/d'êñda; d'êño
                                            B   t'ê'o/tê'ô'da

*d'iid 'to refuse'   R   d'iid
                                            S   diid
                                            B   t'iid/t'iida

*diim, Pl *diim-am M/M 'tortoise'   R   dîm, Pl diim'ãm M/F
                                            S   diin M, Pl diiman M
                                            B   tîŋ M (Ed)

*doon 'to want, like'   R   d'õon
                                            S   doon

*dub 'to roast'   R   dub
                                            S   dub-an 'roasted'
                                            B   tûb/t'ûba

*dundum F 'ant hill'   S   dundumo F
                                            B   tutun F 'ant hill, small hill'

*dûr/d'ûrã 'to play, sing'   R   dur/d'ûra; dûr
                                            B   tûr/t'ûra

*duub M 'hat'   R   dûb, Pl dub'âb M/M 'white hat of dabel elders'
                                            S   duub 'turban'

*duul 'group of spies'   R   duul, Pl duul'âl
                                            S   duul-i 'to attack (of troops)'

*ɗaaɓ 'to leave out'

S ɗaaɓ-i 'to leave out, pass by'
B 'ɗáaɓ/'ɗ'ââɓa 'to leave'

*ɗaa-i/ɗãã-'ica 'to melt (tr.)'

R ɗaai/ɗa'ica
B 'ɗãai/'ɗaa'ia 'to melt fat'

*ɗaac-i 'to fall upon'

S ɗaac-i
B 'ɗê'i 'to drop (tr.)'

*ɗabar M 'backbone'

R ɗ'âbar, Pl ɗab'ãrre M/F
S ɗabar, Pl ɗabarro 'back'

*ɗaɗɗami 'to taste'

S ɗaɗɗami
B 'ɗi'ɗɗ'ime/'ɗi'ɗɗim'ia

*ɗagañ, Pl *ɗagañ M/F 'stone'

R ɗag'áñ, Pl ɗag'áñ M/F
S ɗagañ M, Pl ɗagañ F, ɗagñan F
B 'ɗak'ããce M

*ɗah 'to say'

R ɗañ; ɗah
S ɗeh (Imper.)
B erah (Ed)

*ɗãñàn F 'cold (n)'

S ɗañan F
B 'ɗãñàn F

*ɗam 'to drink milk'

S ɗan
R ɗãm 'to drink milk, blood'

*ɗam-mee 'to finish (tr.)'

S ɗammee
B 'ɗamme (Ed)

*ɗaq-o 'to accumulate herds'

R ɗ'âxo/ɗax'âɗa
S ɗaqo

*ɗaq-o 'to bathe, have a bath'

R ɗ'ixo/ɗ'ixɗa
S ɗaqo
B 'ɗ'â'o/'ɗã''â'ɗa

*ɗar M 'clothes'

S ɗar M
J ɗãr M
cf. R ɗaɓ'ár, Pl ɗarɓ'ô F/M

*ɗarbañ 'to slap'

R ɗ'ãrbañ
B 'ɗarb'âh/'ɗarb'âha
cf. S ɗarbañ

*ɗêèr, Pl *ɗèr-ɗêèr 'long, tall'

R ɗêr, Pl ɗerɗ'êr
S ɗer; ɗerer 'length, height'
J ɗeer 'high'
B 'ɗ'êer

*ɗeg, Pl ɗeg-o F/M 'ear'

R ɗóg, Pl ɗog'ô F/M
S ɗég F, Pl ɗego
J ɗég F
B 'ɗeg, Pl 'ɗ'ege F/Pl

*ḍel 'to give birth'
R ḍel
S ḍal
B 'ḍel/d'êia

*la-ḍel 'to be born' (cf. 3.6.5.3.3)
R lã-ḍel
B l-'ḍel- (E); n-'ḍel-

*ḍeri M 'clay pot'
R ḍ'iri, Pl ḍiri'ŏ M/M
S ḍeri M
B 'ḍerg, 'd'êrgᵉ M

*ḍ'êràg 'to be satiated'
R ḍ'ãrag 'to be satisfied'
S ḍereg
B 'ḍêrek/d'êrka

*ḍig 'to lay down'
S ḍig 'to put'
B 'ḍig/d'iga

*ḍĩig M 'blood'
R ḍĩg, Pl ḍiig'ãg M/F
S ḍiig M
J ḍĩig F
B 'ḍĩig M

*ḍis/ḍ'ĩsã 'to build'
R ḍis/d'ĩsa
S ḍis
B 'ḍĩs/d'ĩsa

*ḍoobo F 'mud'
R ḍõb, ḍ'õbo, Pl ḍob'ãb F/M
S ḍoobo F 'mud, clay'
B 'ḍoobᵉ F (Ed)

*ka ḍuɓo 'to hit' (see 3.6.5.3.2)
S ku ḍuɓo
B k'ĩ-'diɓo/ki-'diɓ'i'da

*ḍuuban 'thin'
S ḍuuban
B 'ḍuua (*b → ∅/V__V)

*-eeḍ 'her (poss.)'
R -ĩc-eḍ-a
S -eeḍ
B -ee'd

*'êrèg/'êrgà 'to send somebody'
R 'êreg/'êrga
B 'êrᵉg, 'êrᵉk/'êrgã

*ɓaḍḍiso 'to sit'
R ɓiddiso (Fleming 1964:70)
S ɓaddiso
B ɓir'iiso

*ɓaħn- 'gap in upper teeth ridge'
R ɓaħan, Pl ɓaħan'ŏ
S ɓanaħ M, Pl ɓanaħyo 'gap between teeth, knuckle'

*ɓal 'to curse'
R ɓâl
S ɓal 'to put a spell on'

*ɓal 'to do, make'
S ɓal
B ɓal/ɓ'ãla 'to make, prepare'

*ɓar, Pl *ɓar-o F/M 'finger'   R ɓãr, Pl ɓarr'õ M/M
                                   S ɓar F, Pl ɓaro
                                   J ɓar, Pl ɓãr-nya
                                   B ɓar, Pl ɓarᵉ F/Pl

*ɓeeḍ F 'rib'   S ɓeeḍ F
                                   J ɓeer
                                   B ɓ'ẽe'd, ɓ'ẽer'd, Pl ɓeerᵉ F/Pl

*ɓeiḍ 'to uncover'   S ɓeiḍ-i 'to undress, disrobe'
                                   B ɓiiḍ (Ed)

*ɓîl 'to comb',   R ɓîl/ɓ'îla
   *ɓil-o 'to comb oneself'   B ɓil 'to comb'
   (see 3.6.5.2.1)   ɓil-o/ɓil'î'da 'to comb oneself'
                                   cf. S ɓeḍ

*ɓîirî 'to observe'   R ɓ'îiri
                                   S ɓüri
                                   B ɓîirᵉ/ɓiir'ia

*ɓilɓil F 'pepper' (Arabic loanword) S ɓilɓil (-sha)
                                      B ɓîɓ'il F

*ɓil- M 'comb'   R ɓilm'ãc, Pl ɓilmacõ M/M
                                   B ɓ'îlᵉ M

*ɓooḍi 'to whistle'   S ɓooḍi
                                   B ɓoorᵉ/ɓoor'ia

*ɓooɓi 'to send (herds) out to   R ɓ'õõɓi
   graze'   S ɓooɓi

*ɓõõl M 'face'   R ɓôl, Pl ɓol'ãl M/M
                                   S ɓool-daqo 'to wash face'
                                   B ɓõõl M

*ɓur/ɓ'ũrã 'to open'   R ɓur
                                   S ɓur
                                   B ɓur/ɓ'ũra

*ɓuut M 'soup'   S ɓuuḍ M
                                   B ɓuuḍ M/Pl

*gaaban 'short'   R gaab'ãn, Pl agaab'ãn
                                   S gaaban

*gaacam M 'shield'   R gac'ãm, Pl gac'ãmme M/F
                                   S gashan M, Pl gashano F; gaashaan M

*gaal M 'camel'   R gaal, Pl gaal'ãl M/F
                                   S geel-a (collect.)
                                   J ĥal, Pl gaal
                                   B g'ããl (gel Ed)
                                   The Boni word is most probably a loanword from
                                   South Somali. The reflex should have been *kaal.

*g'áès 'horn'   R gâs, Pl gas'ṓ F/M
                                      S gees M
                                      B k'áas M 'molar'

*gaiḍ M 'chin'   S gaḍ M, Pl gaḍaḍ M
                                      B kír' M

*gain/g'áínà 'to shoot'   R gân/g'ǎna
                                      B kín/k'ína

*gaisar 'buffalo'   R gas'âr, Pl gasaar'ṓ M/M
                                      B k'íseᵉ F

*galeb, Pl galeb-o F/M 'evening'   R geléb, Pl geleb'ṓ F/M
                                      S galab F, Pl galbo

*gal/g'álà 'to enter'   R gêl/g'éla
                                      S gal (geli)
                                      B kal/k'ála

*g'áràb, Pl garb-o M/M   R g'árab, Pl garb'ṓ M/M
     'shoulderblade'   S garab M, Pl garbo M 'shoulder'
                                      B k'árub, Pl karoobt'ᵉ M/Pl 'shoulder'

*gàrg'âr 'to help'   R garg'âr
                                      S gargar
                                      B kark'âr-s/kark'âr-s-a

*gargar M 'help (n)'   R garg'âr M
                                      S gargar M

*gar-o 'to understand'   R g'áro
                                      S garo
                                      J gor   'to know'

*gât/g'átà 'to buy, sell, exchange'   R gât/g'áta
                                      B kâd, kad/k'áda
                                      J gad

*g'át-ò 'to buy for oneself'   R g'áto/g'áḍa
     (see 3.6.5.2.4)   B k'ádo/kad'ḗᵈda

*gaurac 'to cut throat'   S gauraᶜ-i
                                      B k'úúra'/kúúr'á'a'   'to butcher'

*gaᶜaam F 'hand, arm'   S gaᶜaan F, Pl gaᶜaamo
                                      J gaáŋ
                                      B k'á'an, Pl ka'anyᵉ F/Pl; ka''áan-ta F 'this hand'

*geiz, Pl *geiz-'ṓ M/M 'tree'   R gey, Pl gey'ṓ M/M
                                      S geid M, Pl geido M
                                      J geed, Pl gḗedo
                                      B k'ḗe, Pl keet'ᵉ; k'ḗed-ka 'this tree'

*g'érì M 'giraffe'   R g'éri, Pl ger'ínye M/F
                                      S geri-ga, Pl geriyyo
                                      B k'íri M

giábi 'to break (tr.)'   R *jêbi*
                              S *jebi*
                              J *jâbi*

gid̪ M 'body'   R *jĭd̪*
                              S *jíd̪* M
                              J *jir̪*

giir M 'rat'   S *jiir* M
                              B *shĭir/shĭir* M/M (E)

giit/g'iitã 'to pull'   R *jit/j'ita*
                              S *jĭid*
                              B *shĭid/shĭida*

g'ilĭb, Pl *gĭlb-'õ* M/M 'knee'   R *j'ilĭb*, Pl *jilb'õ* M/M
                              S *jilĭb* M, Pl *jilbo*
                              B *sh'ilũb*, Pl *shilibtãa* M/Pl

git, Pl *git-at* 'road, path'   R *jit*, Pl *jit'ãt* F/M
                              S *jíd* M, Pl *jídad* M
                              B *shid*, Pl *shitt^e* M/Pl
                              J *jíd*

gi^cel 'to love, like'   S *je^cel ahaw*
                              B *sh'ê'el* (E); *sheelo*

gog, Pl *gog-ág* M   M *gog*, Pl *gog'ãg* M/F
  'skin of camels and men' S *gog-i*, Pl *gogag-i* 'camel skin'

goob-lan 'homeless   R *goob-l'ãn*
                              S *gob-lan* 'childless'

goos M 'molar'   R *gôs*, Pl *gos'õ* M/M 'pre-molar'
                              S *goos* M, Pl *goosas* M

gorei 'ostrich'   S *gorei* M, Pl *goreyo* F
                              B *korii; koree* F (Ed)

gôy 'to cut'   R *gôy*
                              S *goy; qoo*
                              B *kôy/k'õa*

gûb/g'ûbã 'to burn'   R *gûb/g'ûba*
                              S *gub*
                              B *kûb/k'ûa, k'ûba*

g'ûgã^c M 'clap of thunder'   R *g'ûgañ* M
                              B *k'ûa'* M

gũnt-o 'to get dressed'   S *gunt̪o*
  (see 3.6.5.2.1)   B *kun^e/kun'i'da*

gur- 'left(side)'   R *g'ûrro* F
                              S *gurey* M 'left-handed man'

*gurei 'to creep (like a baby)'   S   gur-gurei
                                        B   kuri (Ed)

*gut 'to circumcise'   S   gud-i (of girls)
                                        B   kûd/k'ûda

*gùd'ûûd 'red'   R   gud'ûûd
                                        S   guduud-an 'brown'; gadûûd
                                        J   guzuzúŋ
                                        B   kuduud-a

*guuᵊ M 'year'   R   guñ, Pl guñ'añ M/F
                                        J   gûû-ki
                                        S   guu 'long rainy season'

*guur 'to move house'   S   guur
                                        B   kuur (Ed)

*guur-ʌ-o 'to marry'   S   guurso
                                        B   k'ûûrso/kuurs'i'da

*haa 'yes'   R   aa
                                        S   haa
                                        B   haa

*haar M 'diarrhea'   R   ñár M
                                        S   har M 'human excrement'
                                        B   háar M

*haarr- F 'soil, sand'   R   h'árra F
                                        B   haar'êe
                                        cf. S ᶜarro F

*hàb'ăàr M 'curse (n)'   R   ab'âr, Pl ab'árre -/F
                                        S   habaar M, Pl habaaro F

*hàb'ăàr/hàb'ăàrà 'to curse'   R   ab'âr/ab'ăăra 'to insult, curse'
                                        S   habaar
                                        B   haw'ăar/haw'ăăra; hab'âr/hab'ăăra (E)

*habar/habro- F 'woman'   R   maxab'ăl, Pl ob'õrri
                                        S   habar F, Pl habro 'old woman'
                                        J   habâr F

*hafar M 'wind'   R   háfar M
                                        B   haf'âr M

*hal F 'female camel'   R   ay'û, Pl al'õ F/M
                                        S   hal (-sha)

*hamhaam-ʌ-o 'to yawn'   R   am'aaso
                                        S   hamhamso
                                        B   hamaamso

*hand'uur F 'navel'   R   hand'ûr, Pl handur'õ
                                        B   han'ûur F
                                        cf. S ñundur F

*hangaraaraᶜ M 'centipede'

S *hangaraaraᶜ-i*
B *hangᵉraarᵉ* (Ed)

*hangŭri M 'throat'

S *hunguri* M
B *haŋʼŭrᵉ* M (Ed)

*hanzʼuɠ F 'saliva'

R *hanjʼŭɠ*, Pl *hanjuɠʼŏ* F/M
B *hanyʼŭɠ* F
cf. S *ᶜanduuɠ* F

*harmaᶜat M 'cheetah'

S *harimaᶜad* M
B *hǎrmad* M 'leopard' (Ed)

*hĕl 'to get'

R *hel*
S *hel*
B *hel*

*hibʼẽẽn M 'night'

R *ibʼẽen*, Pl *ibʼẽnne* M/F
S *habeen-ka*
B *hawʼẽeŋ-ka* 'this night'
cf. J *hamĩiŋ*

*hor F 'past, first, earlier'

R *hor*
S *hor-ta* 'in front, firstly'
B *hor-tʼẽẽd* 'past'

*horei 'in front'

R *orʼẽi* (adv)
S *horei* 'to be in front of'
B *hŏr* F

*hurd- 'to sleep long'

R *ŭdʼŭr/ʼŭrd-*
S *hŭrud*

*huri 'to kindle'

S *huri*
B *hʼŭrᵉ/hurʼia* 'to stir fire'

*ħaɖʼáàɖ 'bitter'

R *ħaɖʼâɖ* 'bad tasting'
B *harʼẽer*
cf. S *xaɖaad, qaɖaad*

*ħaɖig M 'rope'

S *ħaɖig*, Pl *ħaɖko* M
J *hadĭg* M

*ħambaar 'to carry on back'

S *ħambaar*
B *hamʼãar/hamʼããra* 'to carry'

*ħat 'to steal'

R *ħat*
S *ħad*
B *had/hʼáda*

*ħʼát-tõ 'thief'

R *ħʼáto*, Pl *ħatay,õ* F/M
B *hʼátto* M

ħãwʼáàl/ħãwʼáálã 'to bury'

R *ħawʼâl/ħawʼãla*
B *hawʼãal/hawʼããla*

*ħawaal F 'grave'
    R ħawǎl, Pl ħawal'ŏ F/M
    B hawaal F
    S ħabaal (-sha)

*ħeɖ F 'wooden plate'
    S ħeɖo-di 'wooden dish'
    B her F (Ed)

*ħiɖ 'to close, shut, tie'
    R ħiɖ
    S ħiɖ
    B hir/h'ira; hêr/her'i'da

*ħiiz M 'root'
    R ħiy, Pl ħiy'ay M/M
    S ħidid M, Pl ħidido F
    B h'iid^e, Pl hiitt'^{e} M/M

*ħiiz(iz) M 'vein'
    R ħiy, Pl ħiy'ay M/F cf. 'root'
    S ħidid M, Pl ħidido F
    B h'idd^e, Pl hiitt'^{e} M/M

*ħizz- F 'star'
    S ħiddig F
    J hittig M
    B hiddē F

*ħoog M 'strength'
    S ħoog-a
    B hŏog M

*ħool- M 'wealth'
    R ħool'â M 'wealth, money'
    S ħoolo M 'stock, goods'

*ħoq 'to scratch'
    S ħoq
    B ho
    cf. R ôx

*ħum, Pl *ħum-ħum 'bad'
    S ħun; ħum-a, ħum-eid, Pl ħunħun
    J huŋ

*ħuuri 'to snore'
    R ħ'uri
    B h'ŭŭr^e
    cf. S khuuri

*ice 'she'
    R ice
    S ei; ai; iyâ-da F
    J iyye
    B ii

*ico 'they'
    R ico
    S iyâ-ga M
    J iyyoo
    B iyo

*-iin 'your (Pl possess.)'
    R -iina
    S -iin
    J -iiŋ

*-*iis* 'his'   R -*isa*
                                       S -*iis*
                                       J -*iis*
                                       B -*is*

**il*, Pl *indo* F/M 'eye'   R *il*, Pl *indǒ* F/M
                                       S *il* F, Pl*indo* M
                                       J *il*, Pl *hundo*
                                       B *il*, Pl *inn*^e F/Pl

**il* F 'spring (of water)'   R *il*, Pl *il'āl* F/M
   cf. 'eye'   S *il* F, Pl *ilo* M
                                       B *il* F

**ilem* M 'small boy'   S *ilmo* M
                                       B *ēleŋ* M 'boy' (Ed)

**ilm*, Pl *ilm-ŏ* F/M 'tear (of eyes)' R *il'im*, Pl *ilm'ŏ* F/M
                                       S *ilmo* F, Pl *ilmoyin* M
                                       B *ilm*^e M/Pl

**imit* 'to arrive'   R -*imi*(*t*)
   see 4.1   S *im-an* 'to come'
                                       B *iaad*/*iid* 'to come'

**in'ām*, Pl *alb-* F/M 'girl,   R *in'ām*, Pl *'ālbe* F/M
   daughter'   S *inan* F, Pl *hablo*
                                       B *hablo* , Pl *habl'*^e F/Pl

*'*inàm* M 'boy'   R '*inam*, Pl *ye'ēle* M/F
                                       S *inan* M, Pl *inamo*

**ing'ir* F 'louse'   R *inj'ir* F
                                       S *injir* F, Pl *injiro* M
                                       B *ish'ir* (E); *ishir* F

**inno* 'we (incl.)'   R *inno*
                                       S *innā-ga* M

**k'āālei*/*kààl'ëià* 'come!'   R *k'āle*(*y*)
   (Superlative Imperative)   S *kaalei*
                                       B *k'āāl*^e/*kààl'ia*

**kaati* 'to urinate'   R *k'āti*
                                       S *kaadi*
                                       B *kaad'ē-i*/*kaad'ē-a*

**k'aati* F 'urine'   R *k'ati* F
                                       S *kaadi* F
                                       B *k'āād*^e F

**ka*^c 'to stand up'   S *ka*^c-*i*
   cf. *k'i*^c*i*   B *ka'* (Ed)
                                       J *ka'*; *kah*

*kaldai 'alone'   R kald'âi
                                         B kâl'de'da (E)

*kammis F 'bread'   S kibis F; kimis F 'flat bread'
                                         B kam'is (E) F

*kaniic F 'mosquito'   S kaneeco F
                                         B kanîi F (E); kin'ii' F

*k'âr-î 'to cook, boil (tr.)'   R k'âri
                                         S kari
                                         B k'âre/kar'ia

*kas 'to understand'   S kas
                                         B kâs/k'âsa 'to know, understand'

*keen 'to bring'   S keen
                                         B k'êê/k'êêna
                                         J sheeŋ

*kelei 'alone   R kel'êi
                                         S keli F (adj)
                                         J shêlee

*kilkil F 'armpit'   S kilkilo   , Pl kilkiloyin F/M
                                         B shish'il F

*k'îci/k'îcî-câ 'to wake up (tr.)'   R k'îñi/k'âñca
   cf. *kac   S kici   'to awaken'
                                         B k'î'i/kî'iya

*kob, Pl *kob-o F/M 'shoe, sandal'   R kob, Pl kob'ô F/M
                                         S kab F, Pl kabo M
                                         B kôb, Pl k'ôbe F/Pl

*kol M 'time, occasion'   R kolo, Pl kol'âl
                                         S kol M

*koob M 'cup'   R kôb
                                         S koob M

*kor, Pl *kor-o F/M 'camel béll'   R k'ôro, Pl kôroyô F/M
                                         S kor F, Pl koro M

*kor/k'ôrâ 'to climb'   R kôr
                                         S kor-i
                                         B kor/k'ôra

*kow 'one'   R kôw
                                         S kow F
                                         B kôw
                                         J kow; koo

kuʃ/k'ûʃâ 'to fall'   R kuʃ/k'ûʃa
                                         S kuʃ
                                         B kûʃ/k'ûʃa

*kŭl'ăĭl M 'heat, warmth'   R kul'êl, Pl kul'êlle M/F
                                           S kulayl M; kul M
                                           B kul'êêl M 'heat, pain'

*kurs M 'hump of camel'   R k'ŭras, Pl kurs'ŏ M/M ('hump of cows, camels')
                                           S kurs M, Pl kurusyo F

*laab 'to fold'   S laab
                                           B lâb/l'âba 'to fold, bend'

*lâb/l'âbă 'to return (tr.)'   R lâb/l'âba
                                           B hã-l'âb/hã-l'âa

*lañas M 'well (of water)'   S laas-ka
                                           B l'ãhas M

*lămmã 'two'   R l'ãma
                                           S laba F
                                           J lãmma
                                           B lôw

*laob 'to bend metal'   S laab-i 'to bend'
    cf. *lâb   B loob/l'ŏŏba

*laſ, Pl *laſ-o F/M 'bone'   R lãſ, Pl laſ'ŏ F/M
                                           S laſ F, Pl laſo
                                           B laſ, Pl laſᵉ

*lañ F 'ewe'   R lañ, Pl on'ŏ F/M
                                           S lañ F, Pl laño M

*laᶜam, Pl *laᶜam-o F/M 'branch'   S laan-ta, Pl laamo
                                           B la'an F
                                           cf. R liix'ĩm, Pl liixim'ŏ F/M

*leſ 'to lick'   S leſ-i
                                           B leſ (Ed)

*libaañ M 'lion'   S libañ M, Pl libañyo F
                                           J libãâh
                                           cf. B juw'ã ; juwah M (E)

*liñ 'six'   R liñ
                                           S liñ F
                                           B lĩh
                                           J lih; li°

*loiᶜ F 'cattle'   R l'ŏĭlyo F
                                           S loᶜ F
                                           J lôŏ F
                                           B l'ŏi'

*luqum, Pl *luqum-o F/M 'neck'   R lux'ŭm, Pl luxum'ŏ F/M
                                           S luqun F, Pl luqumo M
                                           cf. B n'u'un F

*ḽuuḽ 'to shake part of the body'   S ḽuḽ 'to shake hand, tail'
                                       B ḽ'ûuḽ/ḽ'ûuḽa

*ḽû- F 'leg, foot'   R ḽuñ, Pl ḽuñuḽô F/M
                                       S ḽug F, Pl ḽugo M
                                       J ḽuᵓ

*maaḽ 'to milk'   R m'âaḽ
                                       S maaḽ

*maaḽim 'day'   R maaḽ'ĩm, Pl maaḽ'ĩme M/F
                                       S maaḽin F, Pl maḽmo
                                       B m'ââḽᵉ F

*mâân-tã 'today' ('this day')   R mããnta
                                       S maanta; manta
                                       B m'âan; m'âan-ta 'this day'

*mágàᶜ; *mâᶜg M 'name'   R m'âgañ, Pl magañ'ênne M/F
                                       S magaᶜ
                                       J magââ M, maɣâ'
                                       B m'â'ag M

*mãñ'ân F 'barren woman'   R mañ'ân, Pl mañan'ô F/M
                                       B mah'ân F

*m'âḽãb M 'honey'   R m'âḽab M
                                       S maḽab M
                                       B m'âḽub M

*mandiiḽ F 'knife'   R mind'ĩḽa, Pl mindiḽay'ô F/M (used for shaving)
                                       S mandiiḽ F
                                       B mĩind F; mĩnnᵉ (E)

*mantaan, Pl mantaano 'twin'   R mant'ân, Pl mantan'ô; mand'ân, Pl mandaan'ô F/M
                                       S mataan M, Pl mataano F

*maqaḽ 'young goats and sheep'   R max'âḽ
                                       S maqaḽ F

*maqaḽ 'to hear'   S maqaḽ
                                       B m'â'aḽ/mâ'âḽa

*maṛ 'to be round'   R mâṛ
                                       S meṛsan, meeṛ-san 'round'
                                       B m'êṛ-e/meṛ-'ĩa 'to encircle'

*maṛoodɨ; 'elephant'   S maṛoodi M, Pl maṛoodiyal F
    maṛoodi   B moṛ'ôôṛᵉ F
                                       J moṛôôzi

*maṛti F 'guest'   R m'âṛti F
                                       S maṛti F

*matañ M 'head'   R mat'añ, Pl matañénye M/F
                            S madañ M, Pl madañyo
                            J mãdi'; madĭ M (def.)
                            B m'ãda' M; m'ãdᵉ M (E)

*maᶜaan 'sweet'   S maᶜaan
                            B ma'aa

*meeł F 'place'   R meeł, Pl meeł'ãł F/F
                            S meeł F
                            B meeł F; m'ẽesh F

*mĭḍ M 'fruit'   S miḍo M
                            B meɽ M (Ed)

*min M 'house'   R min, Pl min'ãn M/F
                            J mĩŋ, Pl minne
                            B mîŋ, Pl mintᵉ M/Pl

*minḍiq'aɽ F 'intestines' R mindax'ãɽ, Pl mindaxaɽ'õ F/M
                            S minḍiqiɽ M; minḍiᶜiɽ M
                            B mine'eɽ F 'part of intestines'; minĭ'iɽ M (E)

*misqañ F 'brain'   S masqañ F
                            B miska' F; mᵉskah F (E)

*mizig 'right(side)'   R miig (< *miyig)
                            S midig F
                            B m'idig

*mog F 'debt'   R mõg, Pl mog'õ F/M
                            S mag F 'blood money'

*mooye 'mortar (for pounding)' R m'õye, Pl moy'ãy F/M
                            S mooye M
                            B mõoi

*m'ũgdĭ M 'darkness'   R m'ũgdi, Pl mugd'ĭnye M/F
                            S mugdi M (Mog)
                            B m'ũttᵉ M; m'ũgdᵉ M (E)

*mulᶜ 'lizard'   R muł'ũñ, Pl muluñ'õ F/M
                            S mulaᶜ M

*nabaɽ M 'sign cut into skin' R n'ãbaɽ, Pl nab'ãɽɽe M/F
                            S nabaɽ M, Pl nabaɽo F 'wound, stripe'

*naɓ, Pl *naɓ-aɓ M/M 'domesticated   R naɓ, Pl naɓ'ãɓ M/M
   animal'   S neɓ M, Pl neɓaɓ M 'one single animal of a
                               flock or herd'

*nas 'to rest'   R nâs
                            S naso

*naᵓas, Pl *naᵓas-o M/M   R   nañas, Pl nañas'ŏ   M/M
     'female breast'   S   naas M, Pl naaso M
                           B   n'ā'as M

*neeẟ 'breath'   R   neẟs'î M
                           S   neeẟ F
                           B   nêẟ F

*neeẟ-ᶴ-o /neeẟ-ᶴ-îḍã 'to breathe'   R   neẟsŏ/neẟs'ãḍa
     see 3.6.5.2.1   B   neeẟso/nees'î'da

*ᶴoo noqo   'to return (intr.)'   R   n'ŏxo; ᶴo-n'ŏxo
     see 3.6.5.3.1   S   ᶴo noqo
                           J   nãqad
                         cf. B   h'ãã-neo

*nûûg 'to suck (from breast)'   R   nûg
                           S   nuug
                           B   n'ûug/n'ûûga

*nuug-i 'to suckle'   R   n'ûg-ᶴo
     see 3.6.5.2.2   S   nuuji
                           B   nuush'îi/nuush'îia

*onkad M 'lightning'   R   anx'ãd, Pl anxad'ŏ M/M
                           S   onkod 'thunder'

*-ood 'their'   R   -îco-oda
                           S   -oo; -ood
                           J   -oo
                           B   -oo'd

*orrañ F 'sun'   R   orr'ãñ F
                      cf. S   qorañ F
                           B   irîî F
                           B   'ŏra' F; 'ŏrah F (E)

*ôy   'to cry'   R   'ôy
                           S   oy 'to weep'
                           B   ôy/'ŏa

*q'ããḽîm, Pl *qaaḽim-o M/M   R   x'ããḽim, Pl xaaḽim'ŏ M/M
     'young male camel'   S   qaaḽin M, Pl qaaḽimo M 'larger male calf'

*qããḽ'îm, Pl *qaaḽim-o F/M   R   xaaḽ'îm, Pl xaaḽim'ŏ F/M
     'young female camel'   S   qaaḽin F, Pl qaaḽimo M 'larger female calf'

*qaanᶴo   F 'bow'   S   qaanᶴo F
                           B   'ããᶴᵉ F

*qããt 'to take, receive'   R   xât/x'ããt-
                           S   qaad 'to take, get'
                           B   'ãad/'ããda 'to take'

*ka qããt 'to remove'   S   ka qaad
     see 3.6.5.3.2   B   kã-''ãad/kã-'ããda

*ꞩoo qáàt 'to fetch'   R ꞩo-x'ât
   see 3.6.5.3.1   S ꞩoo qaad

*qaboo, Pl *qab-qaboo 'cold (adj)'   R x'ŏbo
                                S qaboo, Pl qabqaboo

*qàb'ŏòb 'cold (n)'   R xob'ôb F
                             S qaboob M 'cold weather'
                             B ab'ŏob M 'coolness'

*q'àb-ò/q'àb-đã 'to catch, seize,   R x'ăbo
   hold'   S qabo
                             B 'ŏbo/o'û'da
                             J qob

*qaℓ 'to butcher'   R xaℓ
                             S qaℓ-i

*qaℓℓooᶜ-'to bend'   R x'ŏℓoxe; x'ŏℓoñe
                             S qaℓℓooᶜi

*qanđo F 'fever'   S qanđo F 'shills'
                             B 'ănnᵉ F
                           cf. R xănno 'to be sick'

*qan'ⱵⱵn 'to bite'   R xan'Ⱶn
                             S qanⱵin
                             B an'Ⱶin/an'ⱵⱵna

*qooℓo F 'tribe'   R x'ŏℓo, Pl xoℓoy'ŏ F/M 'age set'
                             S qooℓo F, Pl qooℓoyin M

*q'ŏrⱵ M 'wood, firewood'   R x'ŏro, Pl xor'ĕnye M/F
                             S qorⱵ M, Pl qorⱵyo F
                             J qŏrⱵ, Pl qorⱵnyŏ
                             B 'ŏrᵉ, Pl 'ŏrje M/M

*qor/q'ŏra 'to carve'   R xŏr/x'ŏra 'to carve skin'
                             S qor-i 'to carve, cut, write'
                             B or/'ŏra

*qub 'to pour'   R xub
                             S qub 'to spill'

*quɓaᶜ 'to cough'   S quɓaᶜ
                           B 'ûɓa'/uɓ'ã'a

*quɓaᶜ M 'cough (n)'   S quɓaᶜ M
                           B 'ûɓa'-a M

*qut/qûtã 'to dig, cultivate'   R xût; xût/x'ûta
                           S qod-i; qood-i
                         B od/ŏda

*raaraᶜ F 'bat'   R raráñ'ănyo F
                         B rããrᵉ' F

*raaᶜ/r'ââᶜà 'to follow'   R raħ/r'âħa
                                     S raaᶜ
                                     B r'âa'/r'ââ'a
                                     J ra'; rah

*rȃħ M 'frog'   R rȃħ, Pl raħ'âħ M/F
                                     S raħ M
                                     B rah M (E); ra' M

*rakuub M 'riding camel'   R ruk'ûub, Pl ruk'ûbe M/F
    (loanword)   S rak-ub M, Pl rakuubyo F

*reg M 'man, husband'   S rag M 'man' (collect.)
                                     B rêg M

*ri(z)iq/r'ĩ(z)ĩqà 'to grind'   R rix/r'ĩxa
                                     S ridiq
                                     B rĩi/rĩi'a

*rimai, Pl *rimai-yo 'uterus,   R rim'êĩ, Pl rimeiy'õ F/M 'female camel who has
    womb of animals'   been visited by a bull but pregnancy is not visible
                                     S rimai M, Pl rimaiyo F

*riᵓ, Pl ri-yo F/M 'goat'   R riħ'ĩ, Pl riy'õ F/M
                                     S ri F (< *riᵓ), Pl riyo
                                     J ri

*roob M 'rain'   R roob, Pl roob'õ 'green country'
                                     S roob M
                                     B roob M

*ruħ 'to shake'   R ruħ
                                     S ruħ
                                     J ruh

*rum F 'truth'   R rum F; r'ûn-ta 'this truth'
                                     S run F, Pl rumo M
                                     B rûn F

*saagaℓ 'nine'   R saag'âℓ
                                     S sagaal M
                                     J sagâãℓ
                                     B s'ããgaℓ

*saben, Pl *saben-o F/M   R sub'ên, Pl subeen'õ F/M
    'virgin ewe'   S saben F, Pl sabêno M

*sam, Pl *samam M/M 'nose'   R sãm, Pl sam'âm M/M
                                     S san M, Pl sanan
                                     B saŋ M

*samb'õb M 'lungs'   R somb'õb, Pl sombob'õ M/M
                                     S sambab-ka, Pl sambabbo
                                     B somb'õbᵉ M
                                     J sãmbab

*saríir, Pl *saríir-o F/M 'bed'   R sir'ír, Pl siriir'ő F/M
   (loanword)   S saríir F, Pl saríiro
                                     B sir'íir F

*saᶜ, Pl *loiᵓ F/F 'cow'   R saħ, Pl saħ'ő F/M;
   cf. *loiᵓ   saħ, Pl l'őílyo F/F 'cattle'
                                     S saᶜ M, Pl loᶜ F
                                     B sâᵓ F 'middle-aged cow'
                                     J saaᵓ; saᵓ/loo'

*saᵓa 'morning'   R saħ 'late morning'
                                     S saa-ka   'this morning'
                                     B saᵓ'aa

*saᶜab 'clap of hand'   R s'áħab, Pl sabħ'ő
                                     S saᶜab
                                     B s'â'ábᵉ/sa'ab'ía 'to clap'

*saᶜad F 'time' (loanword)   R saħ'ád, saᶜád, Pl saħad'ő F/M
                                     B s'â'a(d) F

*seeħo 'to sleep'   S seeħo
                                     B seeħo/seeh'ê'da, seseeh'ê'da

*seidi M 'brother-in-law'   S seidi M, Pl seidiyo M
                                     B sidî (Ed)

*sid 'to carry'   R sîd
                                     S sid

*sîi/s'íicâ 'to give'   R s'íi/s'íca
                                     S sii
                                     J sii
                                     B sîi/s'íia

*sízzâħ 'three'   R s'êyyaħ
                                     S sadeħ F, saddeħ F, sáddaħ
                                     J siddíi; siddi'
                                     B siddê'; siddeh

*sîzy'êêt 'eight'   R siyy'êt
                                     S siddeed F
                                     J si'êêd
                                   B siyy'êd

*sonkor F 'sugar'   R sonx'őr F
                                     S sonkor F

*sooh 'to twist'   S sooh-i 'to spin thread'
                                     B sooh (Ed)
                                     R soħ

*sőőr F 'food'   S soor F
                                     J sőőr F
                                     B s'őőr F

*soᶜo 'to walk'

    R soño; soᶜo
    S soᶜo
    B sô'o/s'ôô'da 'to walk, go'

*subañ M 'butter'

    R s'úbañ M
    S subag 'ghee'

*sug 'to wait'

    R sug
    S sug

*suug F 'thirst'

    R sug'úb F
    B suug F

*suum M 'enclosure'

    R súm, Pl sum'ám M/M 'enclosure, fence'
    S suun M 'belt, strap'

*taqsi M 'fly (n)'

    R taxs'í M
    B te'esi (Ed)
    cf. S duqsi M

*tim, Pl tim-o 'hair'

    R tím, Pl tím'ô F/M
    S tin M, Pl timo M
    J tin

*t'iri 'to count'

    S tiri
    B t'êrᵉ/têr'ia

*tol M 'group of people'

    R tol, Pl tol'ô M/M 'meeting, gathering'
    S tol M, Pl tolal M 'tribe'

*tol 'to sew'

    R tôl
    S tol
    B tol

*tomm'an 'ten'

    R tom'ôn
    S toban M
    J tumôŋ
    B tam'ãn

*tuδ 'to spit'

    S tuδ-i
    B tuδ (Ed)

*tum/t'úmã 'to pound'

    R tûm/t'úma
    B tun/t'úna
    S tun 'to grind, geld'

*tum 'to castrate by crushing'

    R tum (of goats, sheep)
    S tun-mi (of cattle)

*tumaal, Pl *tumaal-o M
  'blacksmith'

    R tum'ál, Pl tûm'ále, tumal'ô F/M
    S tumaal M, Pl tumaalo
    B t'úma M

*tuuk-i 'thief'

    S tuug-i, Pl tuugag-i
    J tüüg-i

*tuur 'to throw'

    S tuur
    B t'üur 'to throw on heap'

*tuur 'hump (gen.)' F

    S tuur F
    B t'üur F

*tus 'to show'

    R tûs
    S tus
    B tus'ii/tus'ia

*tVzzoba 'seven'

    R teeb'ã
    S toddoba F
    J tõdoba
    cf. B didd'õü

*uddi M 'dung'

    R ud'ü M
    B uddi M

*uk'ãh 'egg'

    R uk'ãh, Pl ukah'õ F/M
    S ugãh M, Pl ugãhyal F
    J ogãh

*ul, Pl *ul-o F/M 'stick'

    R ul, Pl ul'õ F/M
    S ul F, Pl ulo M
    B ûl F

*um M 'smoke'

    R ûm, Pl uum'ãm M/F
    B uŋ; ooŋ M (Ed)

*ur, Pl *ur-ar M/M 'belly, abdomen'

    R ûr, Pl ur'ãr M/M
    S ur M, Pl urur M

*ur-i, *ur-so 'to smell (tr.)'

    R 'ûri; 'úrso
    S urso
    B h'ã-uri; urso/urs'i'da

*ur F 'smell (n), odor'

    R ur, Pl 'ûrme, ur'õ
    S ur F, Pl uro M
    B ur M

*ürüüri 'to gather, collect'

    R ur'uuri
    S ururi
    B eruuri (Ed)

*usu, *us 'he'

    R usu; us
    J üssu
    B us^e; us

*waah M 'thing'

    R w'ãha 'this thing, this'
    S wah M
    B waa' M

*waħ'ár, Pl *waħar-o 'female kid'   R waħ'ár, Pl waħar'ŏ F/M 'female kid'
  *w'áħàr, Pl *waħar-o 'male kid'   S waħar M, Pl waħaro; waħar F, Pl waħaro 'baby goat'

*wahel, Pl *wahel-o M/M 'companion'   R waħ'ál, Pl waħal'ŏ -/M
                                           S wehel, Pl wehelo M

*wàl'ááł M 'brother'   R wal'ál, Pl walal'ĭnye M/F
                                           S walaal M
                                           B wal'ááł-e 'my brother'

*wàl'áal F 'sister'   R wal'ás-aya (← *wal'ál-taya) 'my sister'
                                           S walaal F
                                           B wal'áash (← *waláal-t) F (Ed)

*wan M 'ram'   R on'ŏ M 'sheep' (Pl)
                                           S wan M, Pl wanan M

*waraaba M 'hyena'   R war'ába, Pl warab'ĕnye M/F
                                           S waraabe M
                                           J waraabã M
                                           B war'áa M; war'áwo-ka 'this hyena'

*waran M 'spear'   S waran M
                                           B w'áran M (E) ; w'áreŋ M

*waᶜ/w'áᶜà 'to call'   R waħ/w'aħa
                                           B wa'/w'á᾿a

*weił, Pl *weił-'ál M 'child'   R wêł, Pl nyáxut M/F 'baby';
                                              wêł, Pl weił'ál M/F 'baby-camel'
                                           S wiił M, Pl wiił-al 'boy'; weył F 'calf'
                                           B 'd'ĕĕk, Pl weił'â M/M; weel, wêsh F

*wein, Pl *wa-wein 'big'   R wên, Pl wew'ên (of living beings)
                                           S wein; weyn
                                           J wiíŋ
                                           B wĭi/wiin-

*w'éznè F 'heart'   R w'éyna, Pl weyney'ŏ F/M
                                           S wadne M
                                           B w'ĕene; w'ĕndᵉ F

*wisiłł-o 'to dream'   R is'íłło/isiłł'ŏda
                                           B wisiłło/wisiłł'í᾿da

*yaħaas M 'crocodile'   R yaħ(a)s'í M
                                           S yeħaas M, Pl yeħaasyo F
                                           J yah'ãas M
                                        cf. B jah'ãas M

*yeeł 'to do'   R yêł 'to make, prepare'
                                           S yeeł
                                        cf. J weeł

*yeꞃ, Pl *yeꞃ-yeꞃ   R   yeꞃy'êꞃ 'narrow, thin'
                               S   yaꞃ 'small, young'; yeꞃ, Pl yeꞃyeꞃ
                               J   yêꞃ, Pl yeyêꞃ

*zeí 'to try, test'   R   yêy
    see 3.6.5.3.2.   S   is ku dei
                               B   kí-dêi

*zey 'to look at'   R   yêy
                               S   day; daay
                               J   dee

*zeyañ 'moon'   R   yeyañ
                               S   dayañ M

*ᶜaanu M 'milk' (n)   R   ħaan'ú M
                               S   ᶜaano M
                               B   aanᵉ Pl

*ᶜab 'to drink'   R   abħûb 'to drink water'
                               S   ᶜab

*ᶜad 'white'   S   ᶜad
                               B   ad-awa; âd(i) M 'white clouds'

*ᶜadaad 'fence'   S   ᶜadaadí 'to fence in with bushes'
                               B   aꞃ'âaꞃ M

*ᶜai 'to insult'   S   ᶜai-yi
                               B   'âi/'âa

*ᶜaidi 'unripe'   R   ħ'êêdi
                               S   ᶜaidiin; ᶜeedin
                               B   eeꞃ'î

*ᶜal'ool, Pl *ᶜalool-o F/M   R   ħol'ôôlo, Pl ħôlooloy'ô F/M
   'stomach'   S   ᶜalool F, Pl ᶜaloolo M 'belly, abdomen'
                               B   al'ôol M

*ᶜaꞃꞃab M 'tongue'   S   ᶜaꞃꞃab M, Pl ᶜaꞃꞃabyo F
                               B   'âꞃub M
                             cf. R   h'âꞃꞃab, Pl haꞃꞃ'âbe M/F

*ᶜaus 'grass'   R   ħos, Pl ħos'âs F/M
                               S   ᶜaus M 'dry grass'
                               B   aasᵉ Pl

*ᶜiddi F 'fingernail, claw' F   S   ᶜiddi F
                               B   idd'î F

*ᶜiꞃ 'rain (light)'   R   ħiꞃ M
                               S   ᶜiꞃ ᶜaddaa gaa 'continuous light rain'

*ᶜol M 'war'   R   ħol   (Fleming 1964:61)
                               S   ᶜol   (Fleming 1964:61)
                               B   ol M

*ᶜoz, Pl *ᶜoz-az M/M 'voice'   R ħoy, Pl ħoy'ăy M/F
                                         S ᶜod M, Pl ᶜodad M

*ᶜŭl'ês, Pl *ᶜul-ᶜules 'heavy   R ħul'ês M 'weight'
    (weight)'   S ᶜulus, Pl ᶜulᶜulus
                                         B ul'ês

*ᶜŭn 'to consume (eat, drink)'   R ħŭn 'to drink milk, blood'
                                         S ᶜun 'to eat'

*ᶜuol 'to be angry'   R ħol/ħol'ŏa
                                         B 'ŭul M 'anger'

*ᶜusub, Pl *ᶜus-ᶜusub 'new'   R ħus'ûb
                                         S ᶜusub, Pl ᶜusᶜusub

*ᶜusuubo F 'salt'   S ᶜusbo F
                                         B us'ŭŭbᵉ F

REFERENCES

Abraham, R.C. 1962a. *Somali-English Dictionary*. London.

_____. 1962b. *English-Somali Dictionary*. London.

Andrzejewski, B.W. 1964. *The Declensions of Somali Nouns*. University of London.

Armstrong, L.E. 1934. *The Phonetic Structure of Somali*. Berlin.

Bell, C.R.V. 1953. *The Somali Language*. London.

Bender, M.L., J.D. Bowen, R.L. Cooper, and C.A. Ferguson, editors. 1976. *Language in Ethiopia*. London.

Bender, M.L. 1971. "The languages of Ethiopia: a new lexicostatistic classification and some problems of diffusion." *Anthropological Linguistics* 13:165-288.

Bremaud, O. 1969. "Notes sur l'élévage camelin dans les districts du Nord de la République du Kenya." MS.

Cerulli, E. 1957-1959. *Somalia, scritti vari editi ed inediti*. Rome.

Colucci, M. 1924. *Principi di Diretto Consuetudinario della Società Italiana Meridionale*. Florence.

Ehret, C. 1974. *Ethiopians and East Africans*. Nairobi.

Epstein, H. 1971. *The Origin of the Domesticated Animals of Africa*, two volumes. New York.

Fischer, G.A. 1878. "Die Sprachen im südlichen Galla-Lande." *Zeitschrift für Ethnologie* 10:141-44.

Fleming, H.C. 1964. "Baiso and Rendille: Somali outliers." *Rassegna di Studi Ethiopici* 20:35-96.

Fleming, H.C. 1976. "Cushitic and Omotic." In Bender, M.L., J.D. Bowen, R.L. Cooper
    and C.A. Ferguson (eds.), *Language in Ethiopia*, pp. 34-53. London.

Greenberg, J.H. 1963a. *The Languages of Africa*. Bloomington.

_____. 1963b. "The Mogogodo, a forgotten Cushitic people." *Journal of African
    Languages* 2:29-43.

Haberland, E. 1963. *Die Galla Süd-Äthiopiens*. Stuttgart.

Hayward, R.J. 1975. "Middle voice verb forms in Eastern Cushitic." *Transactions of the
    Philological Society*, pp. 203-24.

Heine, B. 1973. "Vokabulare ostafrikanischer Restsprachen, Teil I, 1. Elmolo."
    Afrika und Übersee 56:276-83.

_____. 1975. "Notes on the Yaaku language (Kenya)." *Afrika und Übersee* 58:27-61;
    119-38.

_____. 1976a. *The Kuliak Languages of Eastern Uganda*. Nairobi.

_____. 1976b. "Notes on the Rendille language (Kenya)." *Afrika und Übersee* 59:
    176-223.

_____. 1976c. "Bemerkungen zur Elmolo-Sprache." *Afrika und Übersee* 59:278-99.

_____. 1976d. *A Typology of African Languages Based on the Order of Meaningful
    Elements*. Kölner Beiträge zur Afrikanistik 4. Berlin.

_____. 1977. "Bemerkungen zur Boni-Sprache (Kenia)." *Afrika und Übersee* 60:242-95.

Heine, B., H. Hoff and R. Vossen. 1975. *Neuere Ergebnisse zur Territorialgeschichte der
    Bantu."* MS.

Hetzron, R. 1974. "An archaism in the Cushitic verbal conjugation." In *IV Congresso
    Internazionale di Studi Etiopici*. Tomo II, pp. 275-81. Rome.

_____. Forthcoming. "The limits of Cushitic."

Hudson, R.A. 1977. "Rendille syntax." MS.

Huntingford, G.W.B. 1955. *The Galla of Ethiopia, the Kingdoms of Kafa and Janjero*.
    Ethnographic Survey of Africa, International African Institute, London.

Johnson, J.W. 1969. "A bibliography of the Somali language and literature." *African
    Language Review* 8:279-97.

Johnston, H.H. 1886. *The Kilimanjaro Expedition*. London.

Keene, A., and H. Spitler. 1966. *English-Somali Dictionary*. Pasadena, California.

Kirk, J.W.C. 1905. *A Grammar of the Somali Language with Examples in Prose and Verse
    and an Account of the Yibir and Midgan Dialects*. Cambridge.

Köhler, O. 1975. "Geschichte und Probleme der Gliederung der Sprachen Afrikas." In
    Baumann, H. (ed.), *Die Völker Afrikas und ihre traditionellen Kulturen*, Teil
    I: Allgemeiner Teil und südliches Afrika, pp. 135-373. Wiesbaden.

Lewis, H.S. 1962. "Historical problems in Ethiopia and the Horn of Africa." *Annals of
    the New York Academy of Sciences* 19:504-11.

_____. 1966. "The origins of the Galla and Somali." *Journal of African History*
    7:27-46.

Lewis, I.M. 1955. *Peoples of the Horn of Africa: Somali, Afar and Saho*. International
    African Institute. Ethnographic Survey. London.

Lewis, I.M. 1960. "Somali conquest of the Horn of Africa." *Journal of African History* 1:213-229.

_____. 1961. A *Pastoral Democracy. A Study of Pastoralism among the Northern Somali of the Horn of Africa.* International African Institute, London.

Moreno, M.M. 1951. "Brevi notazioni di Ǧiddu." *Rassegna di Studi Etiopici* 10:99-107.

_____. 1955. *Il Somalo della Somalia.* Rome.

Murdock, G.P. 1959. *Africa: its Peoples and their Culture History.* New York.

Oomen, Antoinette. 1977a. "Aspects of Rendille grammar with special reference to focus structure." M.A. paper, Nairobi.

_____. 1977b. "The adequacy of the features tongue root position, high, low and back in a comparison of aspects of Rendille and Somali phonology." MS

_____. 1978. "Focus in the Rendille clause." *Studies in African Linguistics* 9: 35-65.

Palmer, F.R. 1970. "Cushitic." In T.A. Sebeok (ed.), *Linguistics in Southwest Asia and North Africa,* pp 571-85. Current Trends in Linguisitcs, Volume 6. The Hague.

Reinisch, L. 1904. *Der Dschäbärtidialekt der Somalisprache.* Sitzungsberichte der Kais. Akademie der Wissenschaften in Wien, Bd 148, Heft5. Vienna.

Sasse, H.-J. 1975. "The extension of Macro-Somali." MS.

_____. Forthcoming. "Weiteres zu den ostkuschitischen Sibilanten." *Afrika und Übersee.*

Sim, R.J. 1977. "Morphophonemics of the verb in Rendille." Nairobi. MS.

Spencer, P. 1973. *Nomads in Alliance. Symbiosis and Growth among the Rendille and Samburu of Kenya.* London.

Tiling, Maria von. 1921/22. "Die Sprache der Jabārti, mit besonderer Berücksichtigung der Verwandtshaft von Jabārti und Somāli." *Zeitschrift für Eingeborenensprachen* 12:17-52; 97-162.

Tucker, A.N. 1969. "Sanye and Boni." In *Wort und Religion. Kalima na dini. Ernst Dammann zum 65. Geburtstag,* pp. 66-81. Stuttgart.

Tucker, A.N. and M.A. Bryan. 1956. *The non-Bantu languages of North-Eastern Africa.* Handbook of African Languages, Part III. London.

_____. 1966. *Linguistic Analyses. The Non-Bantu Languages of North-Eastern Africa.* International African Institute. London.

Turton, E.R. 1975. "Bantu, Galla and Somali migrations in the Horn of Africa: a reassessment of the Juba/Tana area." *Journal of African History* 16:519-37.

Walz, R. 1951. "Zum Problem des Zeitpunkts der Domestikation der altweltlichen Cameliden." *ZDMG* 101:29-51.

_____. 1954. "Neue Untersuchungen zum Domestikationsproblem der altweltlichen Cameliden." *ZDMG* 104:45-87.

Zaborski, A. 1975. *The Verb in Cushitic.* Studies in Hamito-Semitic I. Warsaw/Krakōw.

Zeuner, F.E. s.a. *Geschichte der Haustiere.* BLV.

APPENDIX: **English - Proto-Sam Wordlist**

abdomen	see 'belly'
accumulate herds, to	*ɖaq-o
add, to	*dar
alone	*kaldai; *kelei
angry, to be	*ᶜuol
animal, dangerous wild	*bin'â M
animal, domesticated	*naɟ, Pl *naɟ-aɟ M/M
ant hill	*dundum F
arm	see 'hand'
armpit	*kilkil F
arrive, to	*imit
back	*aɖañ, Pl *aɖañ-o F/M
backbone	*dabar M
bad	*ħum, Pl *ħum-ħum
bat	*raaraᶜ F
bathe, to	*ɖaq-o
bed	*sariir, Pl *sariir-o F/M
bee	*cinni, Pl *cinniyo F/M
belch, to	*d'êᶜ-ð/dêᶜ-ôdã
belly, abdomen	*ur, Pl *ur-ar M/M
bend, to	*qallooᶜ-
big (of things)	*buur
big	*wein, Pl *wa-wein
bird	*cimbir, Pl *cimbir-o F/M
birth, to give	*del
bite, to	*qan'ʈin
bitter	*ħaɖ'ââɖ
blacksmith	*tumaal, Pl *tumaal-o M/M
blood	*ɖiig M
body	*giɖ M
boil, to	see 'cook'
bone	*laɟ, Pl *laɟ-o F/M
born, to be	*la-ɖel; cf. 'birth'
borrow water, to	*amaah
bow	*qaanso F

boy	*'ínàm M
boy, small	*ilem M
brain	*misqañ F
branch	*la'am, Pl *la'am-o F/M
bread	*kammis F
break (tr.), to	*giábi
breast, female	*na'as, Pl *na'as-o M/M
breath	*neeß
breathe, to	*neeß-s-o /neeß-s-ída
bring, to	*keen
brother	*wal'áál M
brother-in-law	*seidi M
buffalo	gaisar
build, to	*dis/d'ísa
burn, to	*gûb/g'úbà
burry, to	*ñàw'ááL/ñaw'áálà
butcher, to	*qal
butter	*subañ M
buy, to	*gât/g'átà
buy for oneself, to	*g'át-ò
calf-sized animal	*agor, Pl *agor-o M/F
call, to	*wàᶜ/w'áᶜà
camel	*gaal M
camel, female	*hal F
camel, male	*àùr M
camel, young female	*qàãl'ím, Pl *qaalim-o F/M
camel, young male	*q'áálìm, Pl *qaalim-o M/M
camel, riding	*rakuub M
camel-bell	*kor, Pl *kor-o F/M
carry on back, to	*ñambaar
carry, to	*sid
carve, to	*qor/q'órà
castrate by crushing, to	*tum
catch, to	*q'áb-ò
cattle	*loi' F
centipede	*hangaraaraᶜ M

cheetah   *harmaᶜat M

child   *weíl, Pl *weĩl-'ãl M

chin   *gaíd M

circumcise, to   *gut

clap of hand   *saᶜab

claw   *ᶜiddi F

climb, to   *kor/k'ŏrà

close, to   *ñid

clothes   *dar M

club   *bud(-ka) M

coffee bean   *bun M

cold (adj)   *qaboo

cold (n)   *qàb'ŏŏb; *dãñàn F

collect, to   see 'gather'

comb, to   *fîl

comb oneself, to   *fil-o

comb (n)   *fil M

come (Imper.)   *k'ãálẽĩ/kããl'ẽĩà (see 'arrive')

companion   *wañel, Pl *wañel-o M/M

consume, to   *ᶜûn

cook, boil, to   *k'ãr-ĩ

cough, to   *qufaᶜ

cough (n)   *qufaᶜ M

count, to   *t'iri

cow   *saᶜ F

creep (like a baby), to *gurei

crocodile   *yañaas M

cry, to   *ôy

cultivate, to   *qut/qũtà

cup   *koob M

curse, to   *fal; *hab'ãàr/hab'ããrà

curse (n)   *hab'ãàr M

cut, to   *gôy

cut throat, to   *gauraᶜ

darkness	*mʼǔgdǐ M
daughter	see 'girl'
day	*maaɫim
debt	*mog F
diarrhea	*haaꭓ M
die, to	*amut
dig	*qut/qǔtǎ
do, to	*yeeɫ; see 'make'
dream, to	*wisiɫɫ-o
dressed, to get	*gǔnt-ð̃
drink, to	*ᶜab
drink milk, to	*d̤am
dry	*ʼǎngèg
dung	*uddi M
dust	*bood̤
ear	*d̤eg, Pl *d̤eg-o F/M
east	*baꭓi
eat, to	*añam
egg	*ukʼañ
eight	*sǐzyʼèèt
elephant	*marood̤i
enclosure	*suum M
enter, to	*gaɫ / *gʼǎɫǎ
escape, to	*bǎñs-ð̃
evening	*gaɫeb, Pl *gaɫeb-o F/M
ewe, virgin	*saben, Pl *saben-o F/M
eye	*ǐɫ, Pl *ind̤o F/M
face	*ꬵõðɫ M
fall, to	*kuꬵ/kʼǔꬵǎ
fall upon, to	*daaᶜ-ǐ
far	*ꬵog
father	*aab
feather	*baaɫ M; cf. 'leaf'
fence	*ᶜad̤aad̤
fetch, to	*soo qǎǎt
fever	*qand̤o F

fill, to   *búūh̃-ì/bùùh̃'ìcǎ

finger   *ʃaɾ, Pl *ʃaɾ-o F/M

fingernail   *ᶜiddi F

finish (tr.), to   *dammee

fire   *dab, Pl *dab-ab M/M

firewood   see 'wood'

first, earlier   *hoɾ F

five   *can

flash (lightning)   *bilig

fly   *taqsi M

fold, to   *laab

follow, to   *ɾaaᶜ/ɾ'ǎǎᶜǎ

food   *sǒǒɾ F

four   *'ǎʃǎɾ

frog   *ɾǎh̃ M

front, in   *hoɾei

fruit   *mǐɖ M

full, to be   *buuh̃

gap in upper teeth ridge   *ʃah̃n-

garden   *bèèɾ, Pl *bèèɾ-o F/M

gate of animal pan   *aɾit

gather, collect, to   *ǔɾ-ùùɾ-ì

get, to   *hèl

giraffe   *g'èɾǐ M

girl, daughter   *ǐn'ǎm, Pl *ᵓalb- F/M

give, to   *sìì/s'ìícǎ

goat   *ɾǐᵓ , Pl *ɾi-yo F/M

goats and sheep, young   *maqal

grass   *ᶜaus

grave   *h̃awaal F

graze, to send herds out to   *ʃooʃi

grind, to   *tun; *ɾi(z)iq/ɾ'ì(z)ìqǎ

group of people   *tol M

guest   *maɾti F

hair   *tim, Pl *tim-o

hand, arm   *gaᶜaam F

hat   *duub M
he   *usu; *us
head   *matañ M
headrest   *barkey
hear, to   *maqal
heart   *w'ēznē F
heat, warmth   *kũl'ãĩl M
heavy   *ᶜũl'ês, Pl *ᶜul-ᶜules
help (n)   *gargar M
help, to   *gãrg'ãr
her (poss.)   *-eed
hill   *buur
his (poss.)   *-iis
hit, to   *ka duɗo
hold, to   *q'ãb-õ/q'ãb-da
homeless   *goob-ƚaan
honey   *m'ãƚãb M
horn   *g'ãēs
house   *min; M; *aqal M
hump (gen.)   *tuur F
hump of camel   *kurs M
hundred   *boqoƚ
hyena   *waraaba M

I   *ani; an
insult, to   *ᶜai
intestines   *mindiq'ar F
iron   *bir F

jackal   *dawaᶜo F

kid, female   *wãñ'ãr, Pl *wañar-o F/M
kid, male   *w'ãñãr, Pl *wañar-o M/M
kill, to   *agis
kindle, to   *huri
knee   *g'iƚib, Pl *gĩƚb-'õ M/M
knife   *mandiiƚ F
know, to   see 'understand'

lake   *bez F
language   *aʃ M
lay down, to   *ɗig
leaf   *baal
learn, to   *baɾ-o
leave out, to   *daaʃ
left (side)   *bitañ; *guɾ-
leg   *addin M
leg, foot   *lù- F
leopard   *cab'eel M
lick, to   *leʃ
lie (n)   *béen F
light, to   *cit; cf. 'kindle'
lightning   *onkad M
like, to   see 'love'
lion   *libaañ
liver   *béeɾ M
lizard   *mulᶜ
long   *ɗèèɾ, Pl *ɗèɾ-ɗèèɾ
look at, to   *zey
louse   *ing'iɾ F
love, like, to   *giᶜel
lung   *samb'ŏb M

make, do, to   *ʃal
man, husband   *ɾeg M
many   *batan
marry, to   *guuɾ-ʃ-o
meat   cf. 'body'
melt, to (tr.)   *daa-ɪ̃/dãã-'icã
milk   *ᶜaanu M
milk, to   *maal
molar   *gooʃ M
month   *bil(-ta) F
moon   *zeyañ
morning   *saᵊa
mortar   *mooye

mosquito   *kaniiᶜ F
mother   *aayo
mouth   *aʃ M
move house, to   *guur
mud   *doobo F
my   *-ay

name   *mãgãᶜ M
navel   *hanḍ'uur F
neck   *luqum F
new   *ᶜusub, Pl *ᶜus-ᶜusub
night   *hib'ẽẽn M
nine   *saagal
nowe   *sam, Pl *sam-am   M/M

observe, to   *ʃiiri
odor   see 'smell'
one   *kôw
open, to   *ʃur/ʃ'ũrã
ostrich   *gorei

palm (of hand)   *babaᶜ F
past   *hor F
pay, to   *biñ-i
pepper   *ʃilʃil F
person   *dad M
place   *meel F
plait, to   *dab
plate, wooden   *ħeḍ F
play, to   *dûr/d'ũrã; cf. 'sing'
pot, clay   *ḍeri M
pound, to   *tum/t'ũmã
pour, to   *cub; *qub
prepare, to   see 'make'
pull, to   *giit

rain, to   *da'
rain (n)   *ᶜir; *roob M

rat	*giir M
receive, to	*qáàt
red	*gùd'ûûd
refuse, to	*d'ĩ̀d
remove, to	*ka qáàt
rest, to	*nas
return, to (tr.)	*ɭâb/ɭ'âbã
return, to (intr.)	*soo noqo
rib	*ɓeeɗ F
right(side)	*mizig
road	*git, Pl *git-at
roast, to	*dub
root	*ħiiz M
rope	*ħaɗig M
round, to be	*mar

saliva	*hanz'uɓ F
salt	*ᶜusuubo F
sand	*haarr- F
sandal	see 'shoe'
satiated, to be	*ɖ'ềrãg
say, to	*ɖah
scratch, to	*ħoq
see, to	*arg/'ârgã
seize, to	*q'âb-ð
sell, to	*gât; cf. 'buy'
send somebody, to	*'ềrềg/'ềrgã
seven	*tVzzoba
sew, to	*toɭ
shake, to	*ruħ
shake (part of the body), to	*ɭuuɭ
she	*ice
sheep	cf. 'ewe'; 'goats and sheep'
sheep and goats	*aɖi M
sheep and goats, young	*maqaɭ
shield	*gaacaam M
shoe, sandal	*kob, Pl *kob-o F/M

shoot, to	*gain/g'áĩnã
short	*gaaban
shoulder	*barbar M
shoulderblade	*g'árãb, Pl *garb-o M/M
show, to	*tus
shut, to	*ħid
sick, to be	*buk-i
sign cut into skin	*nabar M
sing, to	*dûr
sister	*wãl'ãal F
sit, to	*faddiso
six	*liħ
skin of camels and men	*gog, Pl *gog-ag M
slap, to	*darbaħ
sleep, to	*seeħo
sleep long, to	*hurd
small	*yer
smell, odor	*ur F
smell, to (tr.)	*ur-i; *ur-so
smoke	*um M
snake	see 'viper'
snake, poisonous spec.	*bahal F
snore, to	*ħáũri
soil	*haarr- F
soup	*fuut M
spear	*waran M
spell, to cast	see 'curse'
spies, group of	*duul
spit, to	*tuf
spring (of water)	*il F; cf. 'eye'
stand up, to	*kaᶜ
star	*ħizz- F
star, bright	*bakaal
steal, to	*ħat
stick	*ul, Pl *ul-o F/M
stomach	*ᶜal'ool, Pl *ᶜalool-o F/M
stone	*dagaħ, Pl *dagaħ M/F
strength	*ħoog M

suck (from breast), to   *núùg
suckle, to   *nuug-i
sugar   *sonkor F
sun   *orraħ F
sweet   *maᶜaan
sweel, to   *barar
swim, to   *dammaal

tail   *daíb
take, to   *qáàt
take out, to   *biħ-ì
tall   *déèr, Pl *dèr-déèr
taste, to   *daddami
tear (of eye)   *ilm, Pl *ilm-'ő F/M
tell, to   *ceek
ten   *tomm'an
termite   *aboor M
test, to   see 'try'
their (poss.)   *-ood
they   *ico
thief   *ħ'át-tõ; *tuuk-i
thin   *duuban
thing   *waaħ M
thirst   *suug F
three   *sízzàħ
throat   *hangúri M
throw, to   *tuur
thunder, clap of   *g'úgàᶜ M
tick (parasite)   *cilim F
tie, to   *ħid
time   *saᶜad F
time, occasion   *kol M
today   *máàn-tà
tongue   *ᶜarrab M
tooth   *ilħ-, Pl *ilk-o M/M
tortoise   *diim, Pl *diim-am M/M
touch, to   *dáàr

trap (n)	*dabin
trap, to set a	*dab
tree	*geiz, Pl *geiz-'ŏ M/M
tribe	*qoolo F
truth	*rum F
try, test, to	*zei
twin	*mantaan, Pl *mantaan-o
twist, to	*sooh
two	*lâmma
uncover, to	*ɬcid
understand, know, to	*kas
understand, to	*gar-o
unripe	*ᶜaiḍi
urinate, to	*kaati
urine	*k'aati F
uterus, womb of animals	*rimai, Pl *rimai-yo
vein	*ħiiz(iz) M; cf. 'root'
viper spec.	*abees- F
voice	*ᶜoz, Pl *ᶜoz-az M/M
wait, to	*sug
wake up, to	*k'iᶜi/k'iᶜicâ
walk, to	*soᶜo
want, like, to	*doon
war	*ᶜol M
warmth	see 'heat'
water	*bice(o) M
we (incl.)	*inno
wealth	*ħool- M
weight	*ᶜul'ês; cf. 'heavy'
well (of water)	*laħas
whistle, to	*ɬooḍi
white	*ᶜad
wide	*ballaḍ-
wind	*haɬar M
wind up, to	*dub

woman	*ʾabaʀ, Pl *ʾabʀo- F
woman, barren	*mãh̃'án F
womb	see 'uterus'
wood, firewood	*q'óʀi̧ M
yawn, to	*ham-haam-s-o
year	*guuᵓ M
yes	*haa
yesterday	*eelei̧
you (Sg)	*ati̧; at
you (Pl)	*ati̧n
your (Sg poss.)	*-ah̃a
your (Pl poss.)	*-i̧i̧na

Editor: Thomas G. Penchoen (University of California, Los Angeles): Berber

Advisory Board: Giorgio Buccellati (University of California, Los Angeles): Akkadian
Russell G. Schuh (University of California, Los Angeles): Chadic
Stanislav Segert (University of California, Los Angeles): Northwest-Semitic

Afroasiatic Dialects (*AAD*) seeks to provide concise descriptions of individual languages which belong to the Afroasiatic language family. It is primarily directed toward an audience consisting, on the one hand, of students of one or several Afro-asiatic languages, and, on the other, of students of linguistics. In these volumes, both these groups should find succinct treatises such as to provide familiarity with the basic structure of the language in question in a comparative perspective. Each description will be comprehensive in scope and sufficiently detailed in exemplification. But at the same time the aim will be to cut through to the essential and to avoid specialized argumentation. The goal then is neither to publish a corpus of exhaustive reference grammars nor to provide a platform for the analytical defense of theoretical questions. In this sense the series is properly data-oriented. Though the authors will necessarily be of a variety of theoretical persuasions and each will have his own set of preferences for presentation, not the least important goal will be to achieve as high a degree as possible of uniformity in structure, and in the conventional signs and terminology used. This being accomplished, the reader should have no difficulty in finding points of resemblance and divergence amongst the languages which concern him with regard to some point of inquiry. The term 'dialects' in the series' title refers not only to modern spoken vernaculars but to historically definable stages of any language of the various branches. Publication of studies of as many such dialects as possible would provide, we feel, both an encouragement to comparative work and a sound documentary base on which alone this work may fruitfully progress.

AAD 1 - Berber: *TAMAZIGHT OF THE AYT NDHIR*   by Thomas G. Penchoen.   1973, IV-124 pp., $8.50.

The Ayt Ndhir dialect which is described belongs to one of the major Berber languages, Tamazight, spoken in the Middle Atlas Mountains of central Morocco. The description is based in the main on research undertaken with native speakers of the Ayt Ndhir territory surrounding El Hajeb. – While directed to the non-specialist, a number of points in the description proper will be of interest to the specialist as well: the presentation of noun and verb morphology points up a number of regularities which more often than not have been obscured in previous descriptions. Also, phonological rules are given which account for the major share of morphophonemic complexities. The reader will find in the appendices and 'optional' sections conjugation tables of typical verbs–including detailed observations on the placement of shwa in verbs–, a chart showing the main morphological patterns involved in verb derivation, a description of the phonological rules applying in complex sequences of morphemes of the verb group, the 'basic' vocabulary contained in several well-known lexicostatistic word lists, and a chart of the Tifinaɣ alphabet used by the Tuareg.

AAD 2 - Ancient Egyptian: *MIDDLE EGYPTIAN*   by John Callender.   1975, 150 pp., $10.

This grammar deals with the literary language used in Egypt from ca. 2000 to 1200 B.C. and considered in even later times to be the classical written form of Egyptian. The book is directed toward the general linguist as well as the Egyptologist; examples are glossed and written in transcription and there is an index of grammatical terms and Egyptian morphemes. A comprehensive set of paradigms of both verbal and non-verbal predicate types is included as an appendix, together with an appendix on negation and one on the historical origin of certain constructions. – The grammar contains three main parts: phonology, morphology, and syntax, of which the last receives most emphasis. The section on phonology sketches the laws of sound change to the extent they can be discovered. The section on morphology stresses the paradigmatic character of verb tenses and their derivations. A distinction is made between truly paradigmatic tenses and tenses borrowed from Old Egyptian for quotations or special effect. Following Polotsky, the "emphatic forms" are treated as nominalizations under the rubric "manner nominalizations." Unlike previous grammars of Egyptian, this grammar discusses syntax according to transformational categories. The process of "clefting" interrelates emphatic forms, the "participial statement" and constructions with *pw* + relatives. The process character of negation is emphasized, and the implications of so considering it are developed in a special appendix. A sample text is also included, accompanied by a vocabulary and a translation.

AAD 3 - Semitic: *DAMASCUS ARABIC*   by Arne Ambros.   1977, vii-123 pp., $13.

Based on both previous works and the author's own observations, the grammar describes the Sedentary Eastern Arabic dialect spoken in Damascus. While strictly synchronic and written without presupposing knowledge of classical Arabic, it follows traditional arrangement and terminology as closely as possible without failing however to do justice to the individual traits of the dialect. Appendices deal with 1) the regular reflexes of Classical Arabic phonemes in Damascus Arabic, and rules governing the reduction of vowels, and 2) a discussion of morphological substitutions which cannot be interpreted as describing the historical development from Classical Arabic to Damascus Arabic.

All prices are postpaid. Payment must accompany orders from individuals. A handling fee of $1.00 will be charged to libraries if order is not prepaid. Discount of 20% on all orders received within one year of publication date.
Order from: UNDENA PUBLICATIONS, P.O. Box 97, Malibu, California 90265, U.S.A.

SOURCES AND MONOGRAPHS ON THE ANCIENT NEAR EAST

Editors: Giorgio Buccellati, Marilyn Kelly-Buccellati, Piotr Michalowski

These two series make available original documents in English translation (Sources) and important studies by modern scholars (Monographs) as a contribution to the study of history, religion, literature, art and archaeology of the Ancient Near East. Inexpensive and flexible in format, they are meant to serve the specialist by bringing within easy reach basic publications often in updated versions, to provide imaginative educational outlets for undergraduate and graduate courses, and to reach the interested segments of the educated lay audience.

SOURCES FROM THE ANCIENT NEAR EAST

Volume One

Fascicle 1:   R. I. Caplice, *The Akkadian Namburbi Texts: An Introduction.* 24 pp., $2.00.

Fascicle 2:   M. E. Cohen, *Balag-Compositions: Sumerian Lamentation Liturgies of the Second and First Millennium B.C.* 34 pp., $2.85.

Fascicle 3:   Luigi Cagni, *The Poem of Erra.* 62 pp., $5.20.

Fascicle 4:   Gary Beckman, *Hittite Birth Rituals: An Introduction.* 21 pp., $1.75.

Fascicle 5:   S. M. Burstein, *The Babyloniaca of Berossus.* 39 pp., $3.30.

MONOGRAPHS ON THE ANCIENT NEAR EAST

Volume One

Fascicle 1:   A. Falkenstein, *The Sumerian Temple City* (1954). Introduction and Translation by M. DeJ. Ellis. 21 pp., $1.85.

Fascicle 2:   B. Landsberger, *Three Essays on the Sumerians* (1943-45). Introduction and Translation by M. DeJ. Ellis. 18 pp., $1.50.

Fascicle 3:   I. M. Diakonoff, *Structure of Society and State in Early Dynastic Sumer* (1959). Summary and Translation of selected passages by the author. Introduction by M. Desrochers. 16 pp., $1.35.

Fascicle 4:   B. Landsberger, *The Conceptual Autonomy of the Babylonian World* (1926). Translation by Th. Jacobsen, B. Foster and H. von Siebenthal. Introduction by Th. Jacobsen. 16 pp., $1.35.

All prices are postpaid. Descriptive flyers and information on desk copies available on request.

UNDENA PUBLICATIONS, Inc., P.O. Box 97, Malibu, Calif. 90265, U.S.A.

Monographic Journals of the Near East

General Editor: Giorgio Buccellati

Afroasiatic Linguistics

Editors:

Robert Hetzron, Santa Barbara

Russell G. Schuh, Los Angeles

Advisory Board:

Ariel Bloch, Berkeley

Talmy Givón, Los Angeles

Thomas G. Penchoen, Los Angeles

Stanislav Segert, Los Angeles

APPENDIX TO VOLUME 6, ISSUE 2

DECEMBER 1978

The Sam Languages
A History of Rendille, Boni and Somali

by

Bernd Heine

Undena Publications   Malibu

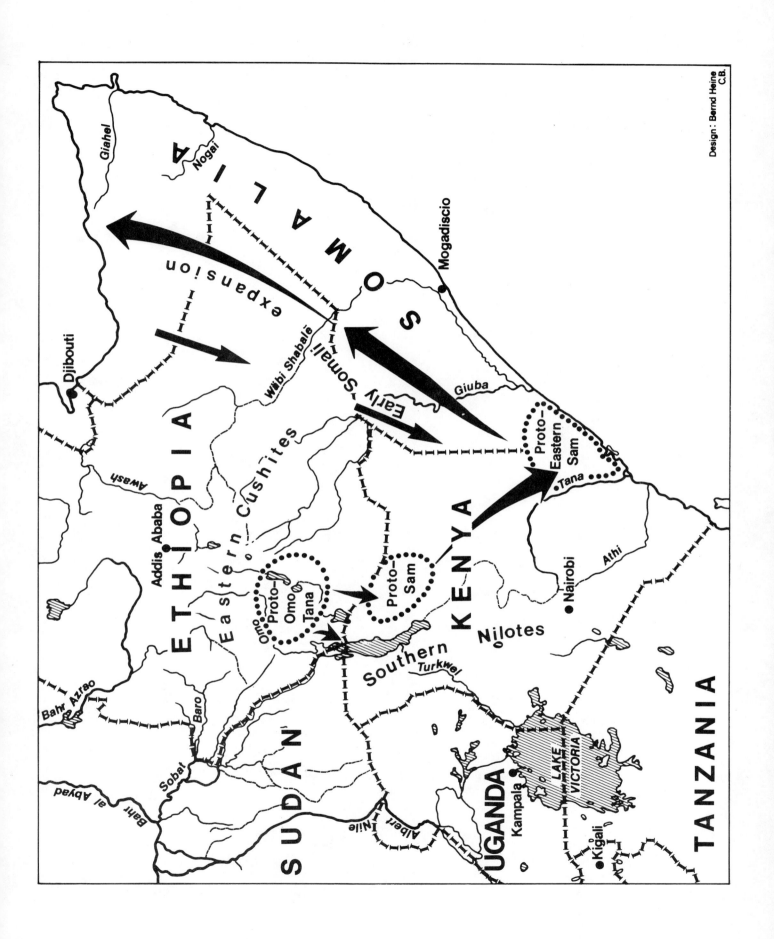